T0315775

HAUNTED
SWINDON
A CENSUS OF HAUNTINGS

HAUNTED SWINDON

A CENSUS OF HAUNTINGS

edited by

Dave Wood and *Nicky Sewell*

Dedication

Dedicated to the hardworking volunteers of the
Paranormal Site Investigators team.
Every pound the authors receive from sales of this book
goes straight to the PSI educational charity.

First published in Great Britain in 2008 by
The Breedon Books Publishing Company Limited
Breedon House, 3 The Parker Centre,
Derby, DE21 4SZ.

This paperback edition published in Great Britain in 2013
by DB Publishing, an imprint of JMD Media Ltd

ISBN: 978-1-78091-362-9

Printed and bound in the UK by Copytech (UK) Ltd Peterborough

CONTENTS

CONTRIBUTORS

We are grateful for the contributions of the following people. Dave Wood and Nicky Sewell's biographies are listed elsewhere.

Peter Underwood FRSA

'The world's leading ghost hunter' – the *Observer*

'The Sherlock Holmes of Psychical Research' – Dame Jean Conan Doyle

Author of more than 40 books on various subjects, lecturer at Oxford and Cambridge and other English universities, also foreign universities; has featured in scores of radio and TV programmes. Website: www.PeterUnderwood.org.uk

Dr Simon Sherwood

Dr Sherwood is a Senior Lecturer in Psychology and member of the Centre for the Study of Anomalous Psychological Processes (CSAPP) at the University of Northampton where he specialises in teaching and supervising undergraduate and postgraduate research in parapsychology and the psychology of anomalous experiences. His interest in apparitions began as a result of a childhood experience with a black dog apparition and he has been collecting cases of such black dog encounters ever since (www.blackshuck.info).

Ken Taylor

Ken Taylor (www.wavewrights.com) has written books on many mind/body/spirit themes, and also writes fiction. He claims no special gifts of a paranormal nature, and attributes his insights to the companionship of open-minded people and enough free time to develop a form of mundane clairvoyance that not only evades fashionable view-points but awakens the mind to underlying, occult and even mystical perceptions.

Trystan Swale

Trystan heads up the Severnside Centre for Fortean Research (www.scfr.co.uk) and has investigated paranormal claims with PSI since 2006. SCFR exists to search for the truth behind a range of Fortean activity in Gloucestershire including ghosts, UFOs and out of place animals.

Hayley Stevens

Hayley is a co-founder of Twelfth Hour investigations, investigating claims of paranormal occurrences, hauntings and ghostly sightings all around Wiltshire for just over two years. The team is based in Bradford-on-Avon, Wiltshire. Her team prefers to take a rational, common-sense approach to investigating the many claims of hauntings and paranormal experiences that come from all across Wiltshire.

Steve and Alison Wills

Steve has been investigating haunting cases in Swindon with Paranormal Site Investigators since 2006. In contributing to *Haunted Swindon*, he is joined by his wife Alison who works for one of the Research Councils.

Dave Sewell

Dave Sewell has extensive writing experience, having been a horse-racing sports writer for a number of years. He admits to having had an interest in the paranormal from a young age, although he is a self-defined sceptic. Dave has participated in PSI investigations in Jersey, Channel Islands.

Malcolm Gould

Malcolm started investigating with the PSI team in 2005 and has co-authored research papers published in *Anomaly: the Journal of Paranormal Research*, and other publications.

Acknowledgements

First and foremost we would like to praise the hard work of the PSI investigation team past and present. Without them this book would not have been possible, and the work of the charity would have failed long ago. The current members of the team are Kirsten Allnutt, Louise Gasson, Malcolm Gould, Clodagh O'Halloran, Dr Simon Sherwood, Shele Simpson, Trystan Swale, Steve Wills and Nicky Wooff. Also thanks to Jo and Andy Butler.

We must also express the greatest thanks to the contributors to this book, all of whom are listed elsewhere. With the exception of those above, these include PSI Patron Peter Underwood FRSA, a legend in the field and a personal inspiration, and Ken Taylor, who has also acted as PSI's history consultant and has provided an incredible amount of historical content right across the pages of this book. Also contributing were Hayley Stevens of Twelfth Hour, Dave Sewell and Alison Wills.

The inspiration for *Haunted Swindon* was the Project Albion of the Association for the Scientific Study of Anomalous Phenomena (ASSAP).

We are also indebted to Swindon Borough Council, who have provided help, encouragement and practical support throughout the project. In particular we are indebted to Councillor Justin Tomlinson, Bill Cotton, Matt Spencer, David Evans, Jan Leard of the Tourist Information Centre, Karl Curtis and the ranger team, Dawn and Roger of Swindon Public Library, Ann McKeown and her team, David Hoar, Martin Hambridge, Martin Rowbotham, Richard Freeman and the other council staff who have helped us along the way.

For their help in promoting PSI and *Haunted Swindon*, we must thank Daniel Garrett of the BBC and the staff of the *Swindon Advertiser*, Brunel FM and GWR FM.

For their assistance in organising investigations, we must also thank the team of the former Pinehurst Community Centre, Andrew Hargreave of Wiltshire Fire Service, Pete Townsend, Joe Tray and the rest of White Watch at the Swindon Central Fire Station, former tenants of the Jolly Tar, David Lewis, Greystone Developments, Nigel Henham; Andy Hill, Darren Edwards and Jenny Kingsbury, formerly of the Wyvern Theatre; and Amanda Loftus and the rest of the very helpful staff of Sally's Café. We must also thank posters to Internet forums and the many other individuals who have provided reports for the book, who are too numerous to mention.

The editors must also thank those who have crafted their journey and views about the paranormal. These include Ian, Rachel, Jo, Mark, Tracey, Dean and the various investigators in Devon, where it all started. Also the ASSAP team including Wendy Milner, the executive and the ASSAP trainees who always challenge us and, in particular, the great Maurice Townsend, who is perhaps one of the greatest minds in the field of rational paranormal research. Thanks also to the many people not mentioned here who have helped PSI and *Haunted Swindon*.

Finally, we would like to extend our appreciation to our respective families for their support and toleration of our interest and research – including allowing us out for a Boxing Day investigation and the missing of several family gatherings due to our pursuit of the paranormal.

PREFACE

In this original and fascinating work, the reader will find not only thought-provoking ghost theories and practical on-the-spot investigative reports but also a wealth of concise census-style accounts of hauntings that are as interesting as they are valuable.

It is of utmost importance that such reported happenings are recounted by responsible and intrepid investigators and the founders of PSI show they are the ideal people to be involved. They have my warmest admiration and support.

Peter Underwood, FRSA
Website: www.PeterUnderwood.org.uk

FOREWORD

What I like about this *Haunted Swindon* book is that it contains first-hand accounts of anomalous experiences as well as first-hand accounts of investigations of allegedly haunted locations. Unlike many other books on hauntings, it is not merely a collection of unsubstantiated reports of ghost stories. It covers a variety of different sites too, from the relatively old to the fairly modern.

In this book, Dave and Nicky have tried to adopt a neutral and scientific approach to these alleged cases of haunting and did not set out either to debunk them or to 'prove' their paranormality. Instead they have considered the available evidence and tried to find an appropriate explanation(s) for it. Wherever possible and whenever a case warrants it, the PSI team prefer to conduct longitudinal rather than limited 'one-off' investigations of locations. In order to conclude that an event is paranormal, one must first consider and rule out all possible normal explanations – which sometimes can be more easily said than done. One must always exercise caution in reaching final conclusions too and ensure that they are appropriate. During investigations, PSI attempt to test out some of their proposed normal explanations for reported phenomena by trying to re-create them.

Given my own particular research interests, I am particularly pleased to see that there is an account of a black dog apparition included in the book. I hope this book will be of particular interest to Swindon residents, as well as those with an existing curiosity in hauntings. I hope too that it might shed some more light on the cases reported here, as well as unearthing new ones that warrant further investigation by the PSI team.

Dr Simon Sherwood

FOREWORD

For most people, paranormal experiences happen rarely, very rarely. Even if you are part of a group actively seeking out weird phenomena, with midnight excursions to sites where anomalous events have been known to occur, while your chances of witnessing something may increase dramatically, you will still spend most of your time waiting, and hoping, and wondering... in the dark.

If you want to collect evidence of that elusive paranormal incident, you can expect your quest to be a very long one indeed. Few professional parapsychologists can afford the investment of time and resources necessary to pursue such a venture, but Paranormal Site Investigators (PSI) made it their mission to fill this gap by applying rigorous scientific principles to all their investigations.

PSI's growing expertise and publication programme is shining a light on some of the pitfalls of paranormal research, helping others avoid some of the more common mistakes. A prime example is the orb, that spooky-looking artefact of many modern cameras, which has been robustly exorcised by PSI's combination of careful analysis and practical experiment.

But what drives people to hold nocturnal vigils in chilly, creepy places? Is it the coffee and good company? An opportunity to face up to life in the presence of death? A desire to help lost souls? The hypnotic lure of the unknown? The intellectual challenge of solving a puzzle? Or simply the innate human instinct of curiosity to see what is out there? The mystery of what happens after death has attracted attention since the dawn of consciousness, but other mysteries are equally engaging (my current favourite, and which always reopens my eyes to a sense of wonder, is how is there anything at all?), so why focus on ghosts?

Perhaps paranormal experiences are nothing but hallucination and delusion, or simply misunderstandings and misinterpretation of very rare events. If so, it is a national scandal that we should be so ignorant, and the sooner we know what is really going on, the better for all concerned!

The stakes are soul-searchingly high. Every effort must be made to ensure fair play in the debate, and part of that policy is the provision of accurate and reliable data. We need to test the persistent theory that says paranormal phenomena are real and revolutionary in their implications for conventional science, and it must be a fair test.

Despite the occasionally tongue-in-cheek portrayal given above, this is a serious task and there is no quick fix. Collecting and assessing evidence gained outside of the laboratory is a challenging task but, just as zoologists must leave the confines of their living rooms to study big game, parapsychologists cannot live forever in the comfort zone of a sterile, ivory-substitute tower. They need to seek out and observe the ghost in its natural habitat, and PSI is steadily laying the groundwork and blazing a trail for this vital and potentially explosive exploration.

Fortunately, PSI is not alone in this exciting inter-disciplinary endeavour, and draws on input from a wide range of interested parties. Indeed, this is a project in which we can all share (just visit www.p-s-i.org.uk to see how). With its combination of single-minded strength of purpose and broad-based support, I cannot think of any group better able to assist in this process of discovery – nor imagine any group more likely to succeed in it – than Paranormal Site Investigators.

Ken Taylor
www.wavewrights.com

INTRODUCTION

In recent decades, belief in the paranormal has probably never been more common than it is today. Recent opinion polls have attributed an open-minded attitude to some paranormal phenomena to around half of the population. Around one in 10 people in the UK even claim to have had some form of paranormal experience.

Considering the almost ubiquitous spread of apparent ghost experience right across the country and across all demographics, it seems somewhat strange that some towns, areas and cities are considered to be haunted and others not. Areas with a long, rich history and sense of tradition tend to be considered haunted, for example Bath or York. Modern towns such as Swindon seem to be overlooked in their haunting renown. Numerous books have been penned on the hauntings of Wiltshire but Swindon, which comprises nearly a third of the county's population, seems to achieve only fleeting mentions.

Perhaps towns lacking in history fail to inspire the imagination? Even South-West Tourism took a gentle swipe at 'towns like Swindon' when commenting on Cornwall's status as the spookiest place in the UK. Indeed, the common perception of Swindon is one of a modern, urban borough with little in the way of history. Swindon author William Morris once wrote, 'in Swindon ... we have absolutely no history'. Of course this statement was written in 1885 and even then it struggled to be accurate!

Swindon as an urban mass might have sprawled from the 'small, hill-top market town' dating back to the Domesday Book of 1086, as it was described by the Great Western Railway team in the Victorian era, but in its ruthless expansion it enveloped – and occasionally preserved – various ancient parishes and villages. As we shall see, these settlements still boast their haunted histories, as do the various ancient towns and villages within a stone's throw of the town.

But what of the *Haunted Swindon* book? Where does it come from and what does it hope to achieve? The *Haunted Swindon* project is managed by local educational research charity Paranormal Site Investigators (PSI), who have been rationally investigating claims of the paranormal across the region for the past few years. Written as a team effort by the charity, the role of this book is to educate. The sheer number of words in *Haunted Swindon* – 70,000 words and over 100 so-called hauntings – dwarfs the majority of ghost books, even those written about larger and more famously haunted places. If nothing else, the mere existence of this book shows that a modern borough, largely overlooked by the ghost writings of the UK, has as rich a haunted history as anywhere else.

The book contains 10 cases of real paranormal investigations at locations varying from a private home to a wood, a modern theatre and an ancient pub. We also delve into several dozen substantial cases that are, as yet, uninvestigated. Finally we take a look at the rich folklore and haunting rumours of the borough. Ethically we have been careful to hide the names of individual living people and the exact locations of private houses. However, more than this, *Haunted Swindon* provides a census of the borough's hauntings. It is not complete, due to the very nature of this elusive and often private subject, but fairly close. Rather than cherry-picking the famous and romantic haunted locations, *Haunted Swindon* provides a candid account of every case. This is supplemented by a rational commentary on these cases; be these major scientific investigations of sites or our own perspective on uninvestigated cases. We hope that by building a census of the town we might be able to answer some questions, such as do 'ghosts' only come out at night? Do only old buildings have hauntings? Does the country have more hauntings than the town? We might even be able to identify the area of Swindon with the most alleged haunts.

The opening chapters of *Haunted Swindon* also seek to place these hauntings in context. What exactly is a ghost? Or a haunting? We do not accept the existence of ghosts with the conviction of belief, nor do we dismiss the subject out of hand. What we hope to achieve with this book is the description of real ghost tales along with the latest rational thinking and ghost theory.

We hope *Haunted Swindon* will provide serious food for thought for the ardent non-believer, the absolute believer, and everyone else in between.

PSI website: www.p-s-i.org.uk
Haunted Swindon website: www.HauntedSwindon.com

What is a Haunting?

Many people accept hauntings simply as part of the rich folklore of our country but, if you begin a serious discussion on whether hauntings exist in some form of objective reality, we are a nation divided. A sizeable proportion of people will actively dismiss the idea as 'a load of nonsense', but whether you dismiss it, or not, it is one of those few subjects that everyone has some form of opinion on. Depending on which opinion poll you listen to, around half the population are either open-minded about the possibility of ghosts or downright believe in them; a startling proportion even believe that they have had an encounter. It would be hard to deny that people – many, many people – have had haunting experiences. But what is the cause of these experiences? The investigation team behind the *Haunted Swindon* project – Paranormal Site Investigators – are unashamed rationalists. As a team we do not presuppose that ghosts exists but we are certainly sure that hauntings exist. This might seem like a contradictory position, but if you continue reading – whether you be a disbeliever, believer, or somewhere in between – you are sure to find some common ground in our argument.

The Hoax Myth

There is a common myth of the hoaxed haunting. Rationally, many of us believe that ghosts simply cannot exist. There are those that believe that anyone who genuinely believes they have had a ghost encounter or compelling experience must be making it up. Absolutely not.

No one can deny that hoaxes do exist, of course, and sometimes famously, but in our experience they are comparatively rare. Some of the very famous hauntings are said to be hoaxes; for example Snopes.com lists the Amityville Horror as a hoax. Often these conform to the journalistic adage that if something is too good to be true, it probably is. Tall tales of ghosts seeking to present irrefutable evidence of hauntings seem often to turn out to be hoaxes. But what of ordinary hauntings: those of homes, pubs, public buildings and places of work? In some cases, attention-seeking teenagers have been blamed for poltergeist cases, and probably justifiably in many cases. Similarly pubs and other public buildings have been known to fraudulently create ghost activity, even in the presence of paranormal investigators, in order to attract business or fame, or even to just have a laugh. *Haunted Swindon* is not going to make libelous comments but those in the know do not need to look a million miles from Swindon to find such cases.

Another category of hoaxes, which seems to have lost popularity in recent years, is the council-house relocation hoax. Certain cases lead to the strong suspicion that the occupants want to be rehoused to a better home.

There are organisations of sceptics out there which, in part, thrive on debunking ghost claims. However, it seems to be rather too much effort to actively go out to find cases and, to be honest, what client would accept them? A lot of the so-called sceptic trade exists to claim that 'ghost footage' or 'ghost photographs' are hoaxes. The glorious thing about the Internet is that we can all examine such evidence. All too often such photographs and footage, denounced as being 'tampered with', are simply the unusual but perfectly explicable processes of modern cameras. There are often no hoaxes; instead just normal photographs that few people have the ability to explain rationally, while lazy-minded people know that it is easier to cry 'fraud' than to do their homework.

So if these ghosts cases are predominantly not the result of fraud, what are they?

The Mental Illness Myth

Mental illness is often second on the list of explanations that cynics find for paranormal experiences. It is, perhaps, most often attributed to the UFO experiencer but is also levelled at the ghost experiencer. If a person claims to have seen a full-figured apparition and one is fairly convinced they are not making it up, the sceptic may point to psychological problems. It is hard to deny that this might be a factor in some cases. Some 'career experiencers' might be fantasy-prone and certainly hauntings have occurred in some cases, even in Swindon, to those with diagnosed mental health conditions, but it would be irresponsible to assume that the state of their mental health was a definite contributory factor towards their reported experience. Again, the rareness of such cases cannot be emphasised strongly enough. Most haunting cases seem to involve honest people of sound mind. So what is the explanation?

The Religion Disclaimer

Before going any further it is probably best to deal with the question of religion. Religious belief – spiritualism included, – is largely incompatible with science. At a stupefyingly basic level, science is about assertions based on evidence, while religion is about having faith with no need for evidence.

It is certainly trendy among sceptics these days to tackle religion head on. However, it is likely done with the best of intentions: such crusaders believe society will be made a better place by the eradication of all forms of religion, including spiritualism. In the case by case analysis of haunting claims, it can be argued that crusading against spiritualism does little good in the investigations involved. It would seem to bring neither wisdom, nor truth, and is more than a little ethically difficult.

There can be little room for doubt that the idea of ghosts still plays a part in Western religion. *Haunted Swindon* is not the place to delve heavily into theology, but evidence, even today, still asserts that the church takes the paranormal seriously. The *Daily Mail*, even in the closing days of 2007, reported on the Pope's order that a new tranch of exorcists should be recruited to deal with such things as demonic possession (often synonymous with haunting cases in the eyes of some of the clergy). Even the church, however, accepts that rational explanations might come into play in many cases. Sources suggest that the clergy consult with psychiatrists before allowing exorcisms.

One type of faith more clearly aligned with the idea of hauntings is spiritualism. Many spiritualists and spiritualist mediums firmly have faith that spirits are all around, and that spirits are the cause of haunted house cases.

For the rationalist purposes of this book, the idea of religion shall be put aside. Our rationalism requires that evidence is key, while faith requires that evidence is disregarded. We know that those of strong faith do report haunting cases. However it is fairly rare for Paranormal Site Investigators (or, a rationalist investigation group) to deal with such cases, as most people of such a mindset seem to require a spiritual resolution (for example an exorcism or clearance). Even if they do approach us we, ethically, cannot pursue a rational solution when they require a spiritual resolution.

Definition of a Haunting

As mentioned, this book starts from a rationalist perspective. Our first task is to explore what a 'haunting' is, satisfying all perspectives. In order to do this the definition must be incredibly broad but, to consider all angles, we must start from a point of agreement.

We accept that most hauntings take place in a context of honesty and good mental health, so this definition reflects that.

A haunting always involves an event, or several events, of one kind or another. You could pick-and-mix any of the following to establish the 'symptoms' of a haunting case: figures seen, unusual smells, unusual feelings, temperature fluctuations, the seen or unseen movement of objects, unusual photographs or video footage, unusual behaviour by appliances, unusual noises or voices, the sense of being touched or watched, and a few less common symptoms beside.

With the risk of becoming unduly philosophical and discussing trees falling in forests when no one is present, another aspect of a haunting is that someone acknowledges it. All the above symptoms of a haunting can take place in isolation, or even in multiples, without being noticed or being described as ghostly. Someone might feel cold and consider it to be a draught rather than a ghost. Someone might find their keys in a different place to where they were put down and blame poor memory rather than a spirit. An unusual feeling might be considered medical by some, and a haunting would not even come into their head.

Hopefully this is fairly uncontroversial, so our best definition of a haunting so far is: 'A series of events that are considered by someone to be unusual and are described as paranormal or similar.'

You might notice that ghosts or spirits are not mentioned in this definition; this is where controversy and disagreements really start.

Why are Hauntings Linked to Ghosts?

The next logical question deals with the reasoning behind linking unusual events with ghosts. It is most uncommon for a transparent figure to emerge and declare itself to be a ghost and speak some truth unknown to the person. If someone sees a supposed figure, why would he or she assume it is a non-corporeal representation of a dead person? Why is a hot or cold spot automatically linked, by some, to a spirit of a deceased person who cannot move on? Knowledge is not innate; everything we know or think has come from somewhere. We are not born with the knowledge of what a ghost is and what it does.

The schema theory of psychology tells us that every new piece of information we receive through our senses is interpreted – and made sense of – by comparing it to what we already know and have experienced. So if someone's keys go missing and turn up in a different room, why on earth would someone assume this was to do with a ghost?

Our knowledge of the world comprises the full range of our experiences, what we have been taught (informally and formally) by friends, family, books, films and television programmes. A person's knowledge of what a ghost is and what it does might be inspired by a personal experience, or the experience of another, or by religious teachings. In most cases, it seems, this knowledge actually comes from the media. Every time we read a ghost story in a book, or read an experience in a magazine, or see a ghost 'investigated' on cable television, or see a haunting depicted on film, this becomes part of our idea of what a ghost is or what events comprise a haunting.

A rationalist would say that a disinterested person who does not think about hauntings and does not absorb information relating to ghosts would not experience a haunting because the haunted interpretation of unusual events simply would not register in their minds. One who believes in ghosts might argue that a 'non-believer' would not experience ghosts because they are 'not open about what to look for'. In one way it all boils down to the same idea: the chances are you will probably only experience a haunting if you know what to look for and are looking for it. This might seem a little too simple – especially considering sceptics who have had a profound and unexpected ghost experience (more about that later) – but on a basic level, it works.

The Context of a Haunting

Virtually everyone knows what a haunting is, whether they are a believer or disbeliever. A person might suspect that a haunting is meant to involve experiencing a cold spot or similar, but people experience these unusual events all the time. So why are these experiences not always reported as ghostly? One formidable answer is that the event must appear unusual and be in the right context.

If one is sat next to an open window on a cold day and experiences a sudden rush of cold, it would be difficult to imagine a person jumping up and crying 'there's a ghost in here' every time a gust of wind comes through the window. Similarly the gasps of surprise at the smell of tobacco on occasion would be less justifiable in a house inhabited by smokers. So an event is only likely to be attributed to a haunting by most, at least in the early stages, if it is demonstrably out of place.

However, why attribute certain occurrences to a ghost at all? Some people are career experiencers and will always attribute experiences to spirits, and others, trained by belief, will do similar. But for most normal folk a ghost attribution is fairly unusual. The context of your environment is of some importance. Certain types of places are 'supposed' to be haunting (e.g. castles, pubs, or buildings that look stereotypically spooky) and some environments might throw one back to a media portrayal of horror film, for example a dark place or a long corridor; or even feeling vulnerable for being alone can make a link – in our brains – between what is happening to us now and what we have once seen on television, in film or in our mind's eye while reading a book. In other cases a haunted context can be created by being told a place is haunted. For example the legends of hauntings of pubs tend to span generations, being told and retold. People that live in supposedly haunted pubs tend to know these stories and can be primed to look out for unusual events.

Such spooky contexts can act as a trigger for us to leap to the conclusion that an unusual event is somehow caused by a ghost.

Trigger Events

It is uncommon to come across a haunting with just one event involved. Usually clients become convinced of a haunting because a string of events takes place, each one building upon the last. The trouble is that when a single event has taken place – for example the cold spot, or an odd photograph – you may start to wonder if your house is haunted. Once a person is in that mindset they, understandably, become extra watchful and begin to notice all manner of odd things they would have ignored before.

Exploring a haunting case often reveals a single trigger event that forms the basis for someone feeling his or her house is haunted. In our experience such trigger events tend to be sufficiently profound to make a person sit up, take notice, and make the assumption that it was paranormal. Less profound events, such as cold spots or keys going missing, tend to lead on from this once the assumption has been made. These profound events might include seeing a figure, photographing something strange, or hearing footsteps in empty rooms.

In conclusion, you might feel you have experienced a haunting if something happens that was unexpected, if something in particular occurs that is stereotypically meant to be linked with haunting experiences, or if you are in an environment where you might expect a haunting to take place.

So that is a haunting, but what about the experiences themselves? Surely the cold spot could be paranormal regardless of all this attribution business? After all, media portrayals have to based on something. If you clearly recall having seen a figure that disappeared, it has got to be a ghost, right? The next chapter considers such evidence in haunting cases.

Is My House Haunted?

In the previous chapter we delved into why a collection of odd events might be called a haunting and attributed to a ghost. So it may be possible for a string of odd events to be called a haunting, even if these events are naturally explainable and nothing to do with a ghost. But if a person has leapt to the conclusion that a strange event is otherworldly, then surely there is a good chance that it is so? Most people who report hauntings are normal, rational folk. Besides, hauntings happen everywhere, in every town and almost every culture, right across time. Surely these events must have something paranormal about them?

This chapter considers a number of unusual events that we have found to be common in the hauntings we have investigated. If these events are taking place in your house does it mean that you have a ghost? Or is something rather more prosaic and xenonormal (the unfamiliar but natural) at play?

Environmental Fluctuations

Hot spots, cold spots and other atmospheric phenomena are often cited in haunting cases. These tend to be supplementary events: they are not the main event talked about by people in a haunted house, and usually act as an aside. Often, such perceived hot and cold spots turn out to be natural and verifiable; it simply is hotter or colder. However, sometimes the cause seems to be an unknown draught or poor construction. Haunted houses often boast a room that 'always seems cold', without acknowledging the fact that the room has three exterior walls. It is not usual, however, to find localised hot or cold spots that are not measurable and are not felt by others. Such cold or hot spots can turn out to be an area of temperature variation in the body or on the skin itself. There are various physiological factors which can cause hot flushes, localised cold and so on, which are well-researched medically and too complex to expand upon here. The crucial aspect of these experiences seems to be that the fluctuation is noticed – where it may have been ignored if a haunted context did not exist – and is attributed to the paranormal.

Unusual Noises and the New House Effect

Have you ever visited someone who lives by a main road and, upon questioning, seems not to notice the noise? Or have you stayed in an old house and heard all manner of noisy pipes and creaky floorboards that the owners seem not to notice?

Our senses are bombarded with too much information for us to possibly process. Our brains automatically tune out information – sounds, for example – that we do not have time to attend to. Our brain knows they are there, but we are simply unaware of them. As I write this chapter, I was only aware of the music playing in the room but, as I stop to do nothing but listen, I suddenly notice the dishwasher, a television two rooms away, a chicken squawking outside and the A419 droning in the distance. However, when my mind is on other things – as most of our minds are most of the time – they simply do not come to our attention.

The one exception seems to be when one is in a novel environment or situation. When something unusual happens our brain thinks we need to hear it. So one might not notice, say, the loud television next door, but if it were to suddenly explode then you would realise it. Similarly, if you move to a house next to a main road, you are likely to notice the constant drone when you first move in but you tune it out as you grow accustomed to it.

Old houses naturally make a lot of odd noises, usually tuned out by the people who live there, but if you are concentrating on your environment for any reason, or even because of a chance event, you can hear a noise that was always there but suddenly becomes unexpected. This can be the reason why a noise is taken for ghostly activity, but how can this be? Surely a pipe cannot be taken for someone banging and surely a creaking floorboard cannot be mistaken for footsteps? Our brain has an amazing capacity to misunderstand ambiguous noises when we cannot immediately see the cause. Psychology tells us that what is in our mind at any one time can greatly impact how we interpret a noise. Paranormal investigators recognise this as half a dozen people hearing a noise and sharing three different interpretations of it between them. Unfortunately, when one is alone, there is no one there to supply an alternative interpretation.

When a person expects a haunting, perhaps because they have seen a television show on ghosts recently, or because they happened to see a ghostly figure the other day, it is in their mind to interpret odd noises in such a way that supports the haunted house idea.

Sense Sensations

A fair share of hauntings presented in this book discuss unusual feelings and smells, the sense of being touched and of being watched or stared at. Again such events often seem to be secondary, in support of the 'main haunting'. Where a person is already nervous and on edge because they feel they have a ghost in their home, they are extra attentive, noticing things they would normally ignore, and are primed to associate these things with the paranormal. Humans often feel unusual sensations, for example ambiguous sensations that may be physiological, and the interpretation of these experiences is based on their prior experience.

Night Terrors

Various ghostly events are seemingly experienced at night, often in bed. Some accounts in *Haunted Swindon* include the sense of being pushed downwards in bed and seeing or hearing odd things. While not fully understood, sleep paralysis is a recognised psychological condition where people are trapped between the state of waking and sleeping, or sleeping and waking, and can be prone to dream-like hallucinations that seem vivid and real. Additionally, when lying in bed, people can experience the sense of being touched. Myoclonic jerks, which are brief shock-like feelings to the muscles, can feel like twitches or the sense of falling.

Movement of Objects

House keys or other objects disappearing and reappearing in another place are a common complaint in haunting cases. This unseen movement is often blamed on the 'ghost', but can be purely psychological. Action slips are common in most people and involve incorrectly completing an unthinking routine task such as putting down keys, opening a sweet and putting the wrapper in your mouth, or going to pick up the telephone but turning on the radio instead. We do this because these tasks are so well practised that we pay little attention to what we are doing and focus elsewhere. Such actions are not stored in our long-term memory because so little attention is given to them. As such, slips are often very poorly remembered. Objects turning up in odd places, then, can be fairly common and normal but only remembered where noticed and considered strange, probably in the light of an already suspected haunting.

Far more rarely are the objects moved within sight. In fact these events are so rare as to be not recorded in any case in *Haunted Swindon*. More common is the hearing of objects moving that should not — such as hearing dishes slip off a surface. People seem to remember the dishes, or whatever, being in the correct place. But again psychology tells us that we are unlikely to remember where we slip up on completing a routine task — such as putting a dish down too close to the edge of a work surface, rather than further back as we always do normally.

Ghosts on Photograph and Video

In the last 10 years the incidences of 'spooky photos' being caught in everyday situations has mushroomed. In the last couple of years, since the introduction of mobile phones with video capability, spooky and grainy film footage is also quite common.

Manufacturers have made modern cameras, especially digital cameras, incredibly easy to use. In fact, anyone can 'point and click' to 'take a snapshot of reality', while having no knowledge

Out-of-focus highlight of a dust particle.

of photography. While this is a great advance in accessible technology, it has become quite a headache for the paranormal researcher.

Often there is a form of barrier of understanding where people believe cameras always capture reality and hence any unusual images must be equally real. Where something strange-looking is photographed, which people know was not present when the photograph was taken, the paranormal is often blamed for the interference. Such mistakes often include small objects just in front of the lens (for example a strand of hair or a camera strap) that appear as massive black or glowing (where a flash is used) blobs or streaks on the eventual photograph. Slow shutter speeds in low light that cause a dragging effect of light across the screen are also seen as evidence of ghosts by some. Finally, orb photographs have caused genuine panic in many homes since cable TV entertainment programmes have suggested they are 'early manifestations of spirit'. Orbs have been studied extensively and conclusively shown to be out-of-focus highlights of light from air-borne particles close to the lens of the camera. Most common in digital cameras because of differences in depth of field, most researchers accept their natural status if for no other reason than the fact that they were hardly ever captured before the invention of digital photography. A full explanation of orbs, too complex to print here, is available at www.TheOrbZone.com

Again, much of the problem comes from the fact that, unless we are primed to expect something unusual, photographs with flaws are usually deleted on the spot and a better version taken. Where there is a 'ghost' to blame, the same flaws are more likely to be printed and framed.

Apparitions of the Dead?

Apparitions do not necessarily have to be of dead people. Crisis apparitions, apparitions of the living and the like, have been reported but are uncommon. Most apparitions, certainly in the case of *Haunted Swindon*, are viewed for a few seconds only. After this they might disappear or, when seen from the corner of the eye, the figure vanishes upon second take. Longer-term apparitions have been reported elsewhere, including those which converse with observers, sometimes speaking truths unknown to witnesses (veridical apparitions), but seem to occur with great infrequency over the decades.

Fleeting apparitions are frequently the trigger event in examined hauntings. Seeing a so-called apparition is undoubtedly a profound experience. After such an experience, an individual might deem their house or workplace to be haunted and start to notice usually ignored changes in their environment unconsciously supporting their haunting thesis as described above. Unfortunately the old false adage that 'seeing is believing' serves to fuel this profound effect. On 'seeing a ghost', many an individual has thrown rational thought and logic out of the window. Such an experience has converted a normal rational person into an uncritical believer. Because of their experience, they can feel a sense of emotional attachment to what has happened, and objectivity and science cease to be a concern.

What are these apparitions, if not discarnate images of dead people? If most rationally-minded people can accept that an odd feeling, photograph or noise attributed to a ghost can be a mistake, how can one be expected to believe that an apparition is the result of some form of mistake or misperception? Surely that is too much to ask?

While these seem not to be a factor in most cases, there are several explanations to bear in mind. In some cases delusion and fantasy propensity are a real possibility: the apparition is purely in the mind of the experiencer. Similarly hoax reports do exist, but are equally uncommon. As mentioned previously, hallucination can be a major factor when apparitions are viewed while in bed. Also rare, but present as a possibility, are the hallucinations that can be caused by infrasound and weak, complex electromagnetic fields. These latter areas of research and their impact on our physiology are popular at the moment, but the researchers involved report that such interference is fairly uncommon, even in haunting cases. In very occasional cases an apparition turns out to be a living person in the wrong place at the wrong time, such as the Hampton Court Palace ghost.

To account for the remainder of apparition sightings, it is generally a good idea to break down the labels and consider what we are actually dealing with. It is a human tendency to apply labels to objects and events rather than being overly descriptive. Various academic studies over the years have supported the idea that memory is fragile and that what we think we remember may hardly reflect reality. One piece of anecdotal supporting evidence from *Haunted Swindon* was of a figure dressed in 'dark clothes' seen at a location that shall remain unnamed. Researchers observed an in-depth discussion between witnesses and it transpired that what had been described as a 'figure dressed in black, seen full on for nearly a minute' had originally been reported as a 'fleeting black mass in the corner of my eye for a few seconds'. These two different accounts are unlikely to be the result of any intention to deceive. It is generally accepted that the brain will reorder events over the hours and days after an experience, so that it fits in with what makes sense. An ambiguous black mass would make little sense to the brain but a figure dressed in black in a building already thought to be haunted might seem to make more sense in a person's mind.

It is surprising how frequently apparition sightings boil down to fleeting, corner of the eye 'black mass type' sightings. Academics at UK universities are currently researching this subject, but it is known that our peripheral vision can easily mislead us and cause misperceptions.

While not enough research has been done into this area, we have anecdotally found that a large proportion of would-be apparition sightings have fallen within one of the above explainable categories.

Unscientific Theories of Ghosts

Numerous books have been written on this subject alone, so it is difficult to do it justice. The following is therefore a brief overview. However, the common theme of most ghost theories is their irrational and unscientific nature. Each one seems to be based on personal experiences, beliefs or nonsense pseudoscience. A rational or scientific explanation requires a model or explanation based on evidence. Unfortunately such evidence does not exist to support the paranormal model, so guesswork and speculation are rife.

Observations of ghost cases have brought about various categories of so-called 'ghosts'. These, among others, include the residual or stone tape, the poltergeist and the intelligent spirit of a dead person.

Stone tape theory suggests that traumatic or emotional events can be imbedded within the fabric of stone and be replayed like a videotape when the conditions are right. This idea seems to stem from anniversary ghosts: an out-of-fashion folkloric tale where a ghost walks on the anniversary of its death or similar. It can be argued that these stories are based on myth and legend rather than any sense of reality. The pseudoscience theory about stone having memory, seems to draw on a BBC TV play, *The Stone Tape*, a 1970s work of fiction, which used this theory. Today the stone tape theory is applied as an explanation rather than an observation. Unfortunately, as there is no scientific model to underpin the theory, it would appear to be just an arbitrary and meteaphorical mechanism to make sense of the unknown.

Another example is the poltergeist. The poltergeist seems to exist to describe strings of paranormal events where objects are moved and general disturbance is caused. To those involved, it seems unthinkable that the events could be mistaken or even unconsciously caused by themselves (psychokinesis). The explanation incorporates the idea that it involves an angry spirit of a dead person. The general intelligent spirit of a dead person seems to apply itself to various haunting cases. Again, beyond the bounds of religious belief, the evidence for such hauntings being caused by intelligent disembodied entities is almost non-existent. Many parapsychologists believe poltergeist cases are caused by unwitting human agents, rather than spirits.

What seems most telling of all about unscientific ghost theories is that they all appear to be rooted in legend and folklore. Are these theories simply the attempts of the modern, curious mind to make sense of the nonsense of centuries past? Certainly it seems a lot of ghost theory was born out of the Victorian period, which happened to be a period when unquestioning belief of superstition was shaken off. Are these theories, also driven by the media, simply a way to make sense of old traditions in the modern world? Once adopted by the mass media, these theories certainly influence the occupants of so-called haunted houses. These haunting cases find misattributed evidence for these theories, and so they are sustained for yet another generation.

However, in such an unknown field it is unfair to generalise. It is necessary to, where possible, examine every haunting case first hand to assess it. Consequently the next question is: how does one investigate a haunting case?

How to Investigate a Haunting

Recent estimates suggest that there are hundreds of groups in the UK that claim to investigate hauntings. For anyone looking to find a resolution for a haunting, it is worth remembering that methods vary wildly between groups. In addition to investigative groups, those of religious or spiritual belief often go straight to a priest, exorcist, clearance medium or similar. However, investigation groups tend to fall into one of several loose categories: the thrill seekers, ghost hunters, paranormal fishers, investigators and researchers. Confusingly, all of these are likely to term themselves 'paranormal investigators', but there are some crucial differences.

Thrill seekers are a type of 'ghost tourist'. At best, thrill seekers spend organised evenings at paranormal tourist locations getting scared and having fun. At worst, thrill seekers will trespass on local graveyards or even find their way into a family home, place of work or local pub to have a laugh, have a drink and photograph some orbs.

Ghost hunters are somewhat better behaved, but more dangerous in a way. Ghost hunters might stay off the drink and conduct themselves in an orderly way, but they still go out, first and foremost, to seek personal experiences. They claim to be scientific but employ the most embarrassing pseudoscientific nonsense. The danger lies in the fact that, with a veneer of respectability, families and building owners are likely to listen to their shocking misinformation.

Paranormal fishers are an ethically dodgy breed, similar to ghost hunters. The anglers will arm themselves with a truckload of ghost-hunting equipment and experiments, and use them to 'scientifically' find 'evidence of ghosts'. Unfortunately the tools and methods they use have no use in finding ghosts and appear to be little more than money-making cons, based on pseudoscientific nonsense. The danger with both fishers and hunters is that they run the risk of making the haunting worse. If families are told that an EMF meter has said there is a ghost in the kitchen, their EVP kit has discovered an angry voice in the kids bedroom and the Ouija board has discovered another few 'ghosts' they did not know they had – suddenly the house is a scary place, confirmed as haunted by nonsense information and the family is in a worse state than it was to begin with.

The true paranormal investigator examines the eyewitness reports of a haunting at a location and attempts to find normal explanations for what was experienced. Further research is then conducted into what could not be naturally explained the first time around. Finally, paranormal researchers are interested in questions that are broader than specific hauntings. They use systematic designs to solve wider questions, often reporting to research journals.

Method aside, perhaps the greatest difference between types of investigator is their ethical awareness. Our researchers have observed the after-effects of researchers adopting poor ethical standards with vulnerable people; the results can sometimes be shocking. PSI observes strict ethical standards, including the following categories of concern: doing no harm, informed consent, no deception, freedom to withdraw, confidentiality, debriefing and responsible reporting of research.

Ghost Hunting Equipment

Scientifically, no one is sure what a ghost is or is not. Pseudoscience has made various guesses, mostly ridiculous, and constructed or borrowed equipment to test the dodgiest of theories.

First among these is the EMF meter. Most EMF meters are constructed to find electromagnetic fields surrounding either mobile phones or power or electric lines. Some ghost hunters genuinely believe that ghosts are comprised of, or somehow feed from, such man-made

An EMF meter – a common but mostly useless tool used by ghost hunters.

sources. The existence of the same haunting claims before the invention of electricity and mobile phones seems not to deter them. Other hunters believe that natural electromagnetic fields have some association with ghosts. While not quite so ridiculous, these theories are likely to be misunderstandings of the seminal research conducted into how weak, complex EM fields cause ghost-like hallucinations. This latter subject is a legitimate enquiry during investigations. The drawback is that off-the-shelf EMF meters are usually entirely incapable of providing such readings accurately.

Further ghost-hunting armoury includes environmental monitoring equipment. It might be a legitimate aim to measure aspects such as temperature or humidity, in order to assess localised cold and hot spots, but unfortunately standard temperature gauges are typically too insensitive, while infrared and probe thermometers, although theoretically useful, are completely unsuited to the task of measuring fleeting ambient cold spots.

Another popular technique is EVP, or electronic voice phenomena. This technique argues that spirits can record their voices onto tape or similar. The technique has little theoretical basis in reality and there are many confounding variables that are mistaken for evidence, including radio interference, normal voices in uncontrolled environments and the internal clunking of recorders with moving parts.

Trigger objects are also used to test the idea that ghosts can somehow move objects. Unfortunately these objects rarely move when recorded by video cameras and, if they do, there are

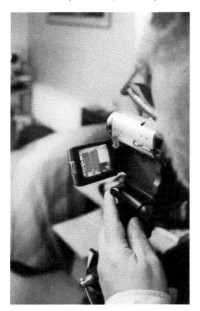

a host of vibrations that can cause the effect. Regretfully, any movement of a trigger object is frequently leapt upon as evidence that a ghost moved the object.

Added to this array of equipment are the good old stills and video cameras. As discussed earlier, hunters with little knowledge of photography frequently make bold claims as to the paranormal status of dust, slow shutter speeds and rogue hairs in front of the lens.

The PSI and *Haunted Swindon* Method
The Paranormal Site Investigators team currently uses two investigation methods: those of the investigator and the researcher. In the first instance, the PSI team only uses equipment matched to the circumstances of the events (be that at day or at night) and the

A member of the PSI team operating a video camera in a private location.

PSI Equipment Officer Malcolm Gould with a small portion of PSI's equipment.

circumstance of the original eyewitnesses of the 'haunting'. Further to this, PSI use rational means to explain any subjective experiences the team think may be possible at the location. While this is a minor method at present, as reflected in *Haunted Swindon*, this method will be refined and become the predominant approach soon.

PSI's primary method over the last three years has been standardised and highly structured. They focus on critical analysis of investigation equipment, techniques and methods. As such, pseudoscientific equipment (such as EMF meters) and techniques (such as EVP, séances and trigger objects) have been employed under controlled and standard circumstances so we can learn the truth about whether these are useful in the course of investigating hauntings. The accumulated evidence of several years seems to suggest that these methods have little or no validity. In the meantime the opportunity has been taken to gather data on the links between paranormal belief, context of the environment, mood and paranormal experience.

In addition, PSI adopts an entirely different, dynamic and ethically-focused method for investigating private family homes. A later chapter will delve further into these special cases.

Regardless of the methods used, the objective of the *Haunted Swindon* investigation cases over the next 10 chapters is to try to establish whether eyewitness and investigator experiences can be matched to find the natural causes behind paranormal events. It is hoped that this will make enlightening reading.

INVESTIGATION OF THE WYVERN THEATRE, TOWN CENTRE

They say that every theatre has a ghost, and Swindon's Wyvern Theatre is seemingly no exception. Despite being a relatively new build, reports of activity abound.

Site History

Built in the 1960s, the development of the Wyvern Theatre and Arts Centre was part of a major regeneration of Swindon's town centre, costing in the region of £625,000. There are unconfirmed reports that a builder died on site during its construction.

The name was chosen as a result of a competition in the local paper, then the *Evening Advertiser*. The theatre was built to accommodate 617 theatre-goers and was officially opened in November 1971 by HRH Queen Elizabeth II and Prince Phillip. Since this time, extensive renovations have been conducted as a result of the discovery of asbestos and the theatre was shut for some time before reopening in the latter half of 2007.

Through researching the history of the site, it appears that the land on which the theatre was built was originally part of the hamlet known as Eastcott and Upper Eastcott Farm. It dictated the boundaries for the development of Princes Street, Regent Place and Regent Street. These areas were predominantly residential and land to the rear of these streets was cleared to make way for the development of the Wyvern Theatre.

Planning the First Investigation – July 2005

The investigation of this site used the group's formal research methodology. A preliminary visit to the theatre by the group's founders allowed them to conduct a thorough site audit where they identified the areas requiring investigation, received all health and safety information, conducted

The Wyvern Theatre in Swindon town centre.

equipment baseline tests and interviewed eyewitnesses. The management of the theatre at the time of the investigation was interested to know whether the group's in-house mediums would be able to relay any information, and it was at this stage that the two mediums attended the site.

As a group, PSI acknowledges the influencing factor that mediums can have on participants if they are in attendance at an investigation. Their thoughts and perceptions can unintentionally lead and sway investigators's own perceived accounts of activity and, for this reason, the group does not allow active mediums to attend actual investigations. If site staff have requested medium input then the group's mediums will visit the site at the preliminary stage.

Following on from the preliminary visit, the group's founders used the information gained through the visit to plan the investigation. There were a number of issues to consider when deciding which areas to investigate, as the theatre is spread across a huge complex with many floors and a large surface area. These factors included recognition of the rooms in which activity had been reported, accessibility to areas, personnel and equipment resources, and the amount of time available to thoroughly investigate each area. It was decided that fewer rooms should be selected to allow comprehensive coverage of each area, rather than many rooms being selected which would have allowed only a very superficial study, from which few accurate conclusions could be drawn. Rooms which were identified as being worthy of research, but which could not be monitored by the team at all times, had video cameras set up in them to record anything which may have occurred in the group's absence.

Witness interviews informed the founders that activity had been reported at a variety of times, across a variety of days, including early mornings and late at night. As the theatre had a full schedule at the time of the investigation, the research needed to be conducted overnight so that full site access could be granted. This approach retained validity as activity had been reported within the time-frame that the team was going to be in attendance.

Witness Reports

Due to the nature of working in theatre, staff turnover can be particularly high. When it came to conducting witness interviews, the founders were able to speak with two staff members to gather primary data and relied on the same two people to provide second-hand information on behalf of a further five witnesses.

A frequent occurrence, reported by a number of personnel, was of the lift being activated of its own accord, and also being redirected to different floors without requests being made. A glass in the bar area had reportedly moved off a shelf, striking a staff member on her leg. The sound of running footsteps had been heard in the administration block, but the source was never found.

The phenomena that was reported time and time again, however, was of black figures being seen moving around the auditorium and stage area and an overwhelming sense of 'presence'.

Medium Reports

As the venue staff had requested medium involvement, the team's mediums relayed to the founders their impressions from their time spent at the theatre. It is important to note that the mediums had had no prior involvement with the theatre, other than being customers, and had not researched any history to the theatre before their visit with the founders.

During their walk around, the mediums picked up on residual energy on the lower floors of the site, from before the theatre was built. They felt the presence of homeless people, from 150-200 years ago; they heard wooden carts being wheeled around; they felt that gangs had a strong influence and they could identify dirty water running through the streets. They felt there was a brewery nearby and there was a young man present who was bullied and was framed for something which he did not do, which led to him being sacked.

In the long corridor, they felt someone had hung themselves in the area and also felt the presence of tramps and a 'cat lady'. They stressed that this was all from before the theatre was built. It was through these corridors that they also detected military activity and could hear the marching of soldiers.

In the stage and auditorium areas, they felt the presence of an excitable group of young people and also felt there was a young man nearby who played tricks on people. They felt he played hide-and-seek and fiddled with the lighting. They suggested his name might be Richard.

On the top floor, a man who was killed during the construction of the site was identified by the mediums. It was felt that he lost his life through a falling accident and he continues to feel quite bitter about his death. They also sensed that he walks around the roof garden area and along the walls before disappearing, making witnesses think he has fallen.

The mediums emphasised that they did not feel there was anything malicious at the theatre and most of the presences they detected were oblivious to the construction of the theatre and those that work and visit there.

Investigators were not informed of medium accounts or eyewitness reports before the investigation, to ensure that they remained unprimed.

Preparing the Investigation

On the night of the first investigation, investigators and staff members congregated in the theatre reception at 9.15pm to receive the briefing for the night. The briefing reminds the group of the agenda for the evening, provides advice on equipment usage, informs the teams of relevant health and safety information and allows anyone to ask questions or seek clarification about the night's activities.

Two teams were allocated for the investigation, each headed up by one of the group's founders. Additionally, each team contained site personnel who were in attendance in both a supervisory role and as a result of their own personal interest. As site staff were not trained in the use of PSI equipment, they were only permitted to report experiences rather than participate in experimentation or equipment use. All staff were fully briefed in advance of the investigation and follow-up support was offered.

The two teams were then allocated their respective equipment, which included electromagnetic field (EMF) meters, ultrasound detectors, humidity, temperature and air pressure recorders and an array of audio and visual monitoring equipment.

It was from this period onwards that PSI has been testing the wide range of equipment which is currently promoted on the market for ghost hunting. After more than two years of intensive research into the validity of such equipment, the group recognises that most of the equipment promoted in the field is unable to effectively monitor and measure what it claims within the area of psychical research. While weak, complex EM fields and the presence of ultrasound may contribute towards haunted experiences, there is no evidence to suggest that ghosts are made of, caused by or influence these fields. Any such claims are nothing more than pseudoscience. Additionally, the cost-effective equipment which makes these claims is not fit for the purpose claimed by the manufacturers. Purpose-built calibrated equipment which can measure these fields is available, but the cost is prohibitive and the equipment does not provide definitive proof that anything paranormal is contributing towards people's experiences – merely detecting fields which are natural in origin but may be experiencer-influencing. When our understanding of what ghosts are, or may be, is so limited, it is impossible to design equipment which claims to detect their presence. Equipment which detects the presence of natural but xenonormal factors is useful, however, as this can allow us to identify experiencer-influencing causes which might otherwise go unrecognised.

Following on from the distribution of equipment, the group embarked on the parity tests which demand the recording of differences between equipment. For example, if a spot thermometer gun is being used by both teams then the investigators allocated to that piece of equipment would point, in turn, their gun's beam at a defined spot of the wall to record its reading. Any difference between the readings is recorded so that the difference can be recognised and any adjustments in the interpretation of results can be made. From this point on, it is essential that equipment is not switched between teams and that equipment is not substituted for alternate models.

With the briefing completed and parity tests conducted, it was time for the teams to commence the extraneous factors audit (EFA) and baseline tests. During this time, the groups visited each of the areas that were going to be studied over the course of the investigation and attempted to identify anything which could lead to anomalous equipment readings or interfere with audio and visual recordings. Things identified included fire exits, smoke detectors, power points, radiators, reflective surfaces and nearby traffic and people. All of these things had the potential to affect results so their early identification was crucial. This ensured that no time was wasted trying to identify such causes during the investigation and, by noting them down in meticulous detail, they could be referred to during analysis.

The taking of baseline readings went some way towards identifying a norm for each area but it is recognised that, in order to ascertain a true norm, many such readings would be required to be taken over a long period of time. The readings taken for this baseline could, in themselves, be anomalous. Similarly, the natural state of buildings does subtly change over short periods of time, so the ongoing baseline readings that were taken throughout the night cannot be viewed in isolation, but as a progression from prior readings.

The First Investigation

After the completion of the EFA and baseline tests, the two teams met on the theatre's stage to start the night with an opening séance. While the group does not adopt spiritualist methods, the opening séance is conducted to allow the group the chance to gather their focus and concentration for the night ahead.

During this first séance, 18 reports were made in 27 minutes by investigators and site staff. These reports included seeing a moving white light and a moving blue light, the sensation of a breeze and several accounts of a black figure being seen on the stage. The investigators were not aware of previous accounts of activity at the site but the site staff were. This is of interest as the reports made, which tallied with previous reports, were made predominantly by site personnel; this could suggest that primed expectation and prior knowledge contributed towards these experiences, which were not objectively verified.

Following on from the séance, the group split into their two teams and the study of the theatre commenced. The areas that the teams were researching were the auditorium, the LX room, the long corridor, the dance studio and the prop room.

The staff corridors underneath the theatre.

The Auditorium

During the sessions held by the two teams in the auditorium and stage areas, much of the activity reported reflected the activity reported during the initial séance. This included seeing moving white lights and the perception of a figure moving around on stage. A male presence was detected and two investigators picked up on two male names – Nick and William. A chill was felt by one investigator, the sound of a door closing was heard, and voices and singing were also reported.

The LX Room

More moving lights and cool breezes were reported in the LX Room. This was accompanied by the perceived presence of a mischievous child and the sensation of something brushing against one of the investigator's legs.

The Long Corridor

Aside from some power drain on equipment, the only other report was one investigator feeling that someone had planned to take their own life in the area.

The Dance Studio

In the dance studio, a clap was heard coming from the adjoining corridor along with what sounded like a child's mechanical toy. The nearby drinks dispenser was thought to be the cause. One investigator reported having strong, stabbing head pains and also perceived the movement of black balls of light. Power fluctuations on equipment were also reported in this area. The sensation of someone spinning around the room was felt by one investigator; however, this could be the result of the investigator knowing what the room was used for (a dance studio).

The Prop Room

During a session in the prop room, one investigator reported seeing someone standing next to her. However, this was not verified by any other investigators, nor was it picked up on camera. As the room was dotted with a wide range of theatrical props at the time, it is possible that one of these could have been misinterpreted as being a person. A dull glow was seen by the group near to the door but it was thought that the light switch was probably responsible. Additionally, from the prop room, the green room door was heard to slam while there was nobody in the vicinity.

Due to the range of activity reported over the course of this investigation, the team decided that a return visit was warranted. The analysis of both investigations will be considered together at the end of this chapter.

The Return Visit

The group's second investigation reflected the initial one in regard to methodology used and areas under study. One area (the dance studio) was omitted due to access restrictions. The purpose of this night's research was to attempt to identify possible causes of the phenomena previously identified.

The Auditorium

Both séances were again held in this area to reflect the initial investigation. In the first night of research, the phenomena reported was primarily visual in nature but, during this investigation, it was predominantly auditory. Clicks, humming, clatters, bangs and thumps were all reported during both séance sessions. A calling-out experiment was conducted where questions were posed and responses were sought. When asked if there was a man present, a click was heard to come from the centre of the stage. On request, noises were heard coming from both stage left and stage right. Movement at the back of the auditorium was heard, after asking if the person present had previously worked here. A click followed by the sound of a door slamming was the response received during the procedure.

During investigation sessions in the auditorium, the auditory phenomena continued and included taps, clicks and the sound of footsteps. A black shadow was seen by one investigator to cross the stage and the name Steve, along with the year 1953, was picked up.

The Green Room
A distant bang and the sound of high heels were heard from, but not in, the green room. One investigator reported feeling a physical tug on their arm during this session.

The LX Room
Knocks, clicks and taps were also heard during sessions in this room. One investigator reported that they thought they had caught a glimpse of somebody sitting on a box, and another investigator perceived the presence of a small boy hiding in the room. The lights from the adjoining corridor were seen, by investigators, to dip in brightness.

The prop room was one of the areas under investigation.

The Prop Room

A metallic rattling sound was heard in the prop room but this was identified as being caused by the fridges and freezers at the rear of the room, which had not been present during the previous investigation. The sound of nearby footsteps was also reported during these sessions, but coming from the neighbouring corridor.

Analysis of the Investigations

The analysis of investigations always demands much more time than the time spent in the investigations themselves. After drawing together all video footage, audio recordings, photographs, equipment readings and eyewitness reports, experienced analysts embark on the painstaking task of attempting to identify correlations between reports and data and to isolate potential causes of anomalous readings and witness testimony.

Mediums' Evidence

As previously stated, information with which our mediums provide us is of interest to the team but is treated with due caution. Mediumship is an unscientific ability, which cannot offer any degree of certainty. As a group we are interested in the phenomenon, but believe that it needs independent study away from the investigation environment to test its validity and repeatability.

There were two points from the mediums' account which the group has been able to tally up to verifiable information. Firstly, the mediums identified the presence of a man killed on site during building work. Reports, albeit anecdotal, do show that a man did lose his life during the construction of the theatre. Secondly, they identified a group of cheerful young adults. Theatre staff were able to confirm that, on the day of the mediums' visit, there had been a workshop earlier in the day which was attended by young people.

Analysis of Investigators' Reports

In the initial investigation, many of the reports made in the auditorium and stage areas were visual in nature and consisted primarily of the perceived images of people or shadows of human form moving around this area. During this first investigation, the majority of these reports came from site staff, all of whom knew what occurred at the site and were therefore primed as to what to possibly experience. Reports were also made by unprimed investigators, but they may have been influenced by the staff reports. During the second investigation no staff were present and only one report was made of a human form moving on the stage. This report and, indeed, those made during the initial investigation were not objectively verified through video or photographic footage and may have been the result of hallucination or misinterpretation.

During the second investigation of the auditorium and stage, the majority of reports made were from the auditory field, consisting of taps, clicks and bangs. There are several possible causes for these reports. Firstly, at the time of the return visit, the theatre was and had been shut for some time as a result of the discovery of asbestos. As no staff, actors or customers had been frequenting this area, many of the sounds heard could have been the result of the building responding to the movement of investigators, by floorboards resettling, electrics being used for the first time in a while and disused fixtures being utilised by investigators. The second possible cause is the new house effect – the theory that a novel environment elicits more reports from investigators than a well-known site as they are not yet used to the building's natural noises. Although the team had

Former staff had reported 'experiences' in the LX Room.

visited previously, two years earlier, the visit was not recent enough to prevent this phenomenon as the investigators were not sufficiently familiarised with the building. The fact that investigators did not report the sounds during the first investigation could suggest that the sounds were not present, that investigators were too embroiled in the array of visual phenomena being reported, or that they failed to report them as they accepted that the sounds were natural, especially as the site staff did not respond to them.

The response of clicks and taps to investigators' questions during the second investigation must not be thought to be indicative of spirit communication. Due to the vast quantity of sounds heard during that session, one must consider the very likely possibility that the perceived responses were chance or coincidence. There were not enough trials to effectively test whether the responses were anything more than chance timing.

The perception of seeing moving lights in the auditorium is a common report made in investigations and may be due to ideoretinal light, which occurs when static light sources are perceived to be moving. This is normally a result of a medical condition causing involuntary eye-rolling, but the effect is commonly reproduced in investigators who may be suffering the effects of tiredness. Sheriff's (1935) seminal work into the auto-kinetic effect may also be a contributing factor. This research showed that when participants are in darkness in a novel environment, where they are unable to locate the source of the light, they often perceive the light to be moving as they have no point of reference for its source. The static lights in this case could have included sensors, fire alarms and smoke detectors.

The reports which were made relating to hearing voices in the auditorium and corridor areas could possibly have emanated from outside as this part of the theatre is located by a busy thoroughfare with many pub and club-goers walking by.

The knocks and clicks heard in the LX Room are possibly a result of it being used for the first time in a while, as discussed in the auditorium analysis. The report of someone being seen sat on a box was only a fleeting sighting and may have been caused by misattribution, as a result of being in an unknown environment where the natural fall of shadows and so on were unfamiliar to the percipient. However, this was not captured on video or photograph and, as it was only witnessed by one investigator, it is difficult to analyse further. The perception of a child hiding in this room during the second investigation correlates with the sensation of a mischievous child being present, as detected in the first investigation. It is possible that the investigator making the report was primed by the report from the previous investigation, which they would have been aware of by the time of the second night. As sensitive perceptions are impossible to measure, the reports remain of interest but no conclusions can be drawn. While in the LX room investigators reported seeing the lights dip in the adjoining corridor. Again, this was not caught on camera and may be the result of investigators' eyes adjusting to low light conditions. The sensation of something brushing one investigator's leg may have been caused by a muscle spasm in their leg or they may have accidentally brushed against something in the room that they could not immediately identify due to the light conditions. The doubt which low light conditions can cause adds weight to the questionable method of investigating in the dark, but in this case it was deemed justifiable for the sake of ecological validity.

As previously mentioned, the clap and mechanical sound heard in the dance studio were identified as being caused by the nearby drinks machine. This highlighted the importance of having a thorough understanding of the venue that you are investigating and responding to the phenomena as they occur. The investigator who experienced strong head pains and the movement of black balls across their vision is known to suffer from migraine, so this incident may have been physiological in nature. It was also this investigator who experienced the sensation of spinning around the room. The sensation may have been mistaken for dizziness as a result of head pains, or the investigator may have been primed towards this sensation with the knowledge that it was a dance studio. The fluctuation of power on equipment is another relatively common report made during investigations and is often caused by low temperatures or disparity in the brand and freshness of the batteries used to operate the equipment.

The perception of seeing a person in the prop room was possibly caused by a theatrical prop in the room, as already proposed. As the room was relatively unknown to the investigator and as it has a very unusual layout with varying levels of ceiling height, shadows do fall unnaturally in this room and this could easily have led to a misperception. The sound of falling footsteps, as also reported from the green room, could have been caused by theatre personnel who were working in the building at the time.

The feeling of being tugged in the green room may have been physiological in nature as a result of a muscle spasm or a myoclonic jerk, which can occur if somebody is tired and slips into a microsleep or brief sleep period and awakens with a jerk. An incident in the green room, that we have not yet covered, was reported by two investigators who had set up a lock-off camera in the room. As they left they turned the light off, but on returning to collect the camera they discovered the light was on. This was captured on camera, but as the light switch itself was not in the picture then we cannot draw any conclusions as to the cause of this phenomenon. It is possible that they had not fully depressed the light switch, and it slipped back on after they had left, or that theatre staff inadvertently entered the room, switched the light on, saw it was a research area and left without turning off the light. However, the latter is a less likely possibility as no sound of the door opening or closing was picked up by the camera after the investigators had left the scene.

Just before we leave the analysis of investigators' experiences, it is worth considering the effect of paranormal belief levels on the quantity of reports made by individual investigators. Paranormal belief levels are measured before the start of every investigation and, over the course of these two investigations, significantly more reports of perceived phenomena were made by investigators with higher reported levels of paranormal belief compared to investigators with lower levels. There are two contributory theories that help explain why this may occur. The first theory suggests that those with high levels of paranormal belief make more reports because they want to experience more and may be greater victims of expectation than their less-believing colleagues. This heightened level of arousal may lead them to misattribute natural phenomena as being anomalous. The second theory suggests that 'spirits' prefer to make themselves known to believers rather than those of a more sceptical disposition as they know they will get greater acknowledgement and acceptance from them.

Analysing the footage
Photographic and video footage have the potential to go through two stages of analysis. At the first stage, all anomalous photographs are identified and analysed by an experienced analyst. Any photographs that go through this stage and still cannot be explained by the analyst go onto second-stage analysis, where three analysts review the footage and explore possible causes.

Footage from the Wyvern Theatre investigations contained many anomalies but the vast majority of these were successfully identified as being caused by dust, equipment and known light sources. There was some evidence, however, that withstood the first stage of analysis. The appearance of a light, on video footage taken in the prop room, fell at the second stage as it was identified as being caused by the light in the adjoining corridor. A 'tail' which appeared to come out of an orb (out-of-focus highlight of a dust particle) on a photograph was shown to be caused by the reflection of the camera flash on the background material. A second photograph which seemed to show the ghostly image of a man hunched over a cane was later proven to be the shadow of an investigator leaning over a chair!

Environmental Analysis

Over the course of the two studies, many baseline readings were taken with the range of equipment deployed. There were, however, few erroneous readings.

There was one isolated case of an EMF meter reading of 5mg for which no obvious source could be identified. This occurred in the centre of the dance studio and a further five baseline tests in this area failed to replicate the reading. It has been agreed by the group that this was probably a fluke reading caused by equipment malfunction or ineffective operation of the meter. Furthermore, there was no increase in perceived paranormal activity at the time of the reading so this, along with a whole host of other evidence (or lack of), challenges the tenacious paranormal theory of EMF readings relating in any way to the paranormal.

The second erroneous reading was by the negative ion detector in the dance studio. This reading occurred in isolation and no increase in activity was reported at the time. It is thought that the reading was caused by a natural build up of static, as a result of the presence of active people in the room.

Conclusion

The group felt privileged to be granted access to the theatre and were grateful for the assistance provided by all staff members involved. Many of the reports made during the course of the two investigations have been successfully explained, but many do rely on our limited understanding of the psychology of anomalous experience, as well as our understanding of group and social psychology.

The main reports made by staff, which had initiated the investigations, had been in relation to the movement of figures in the auditorium and the misdirection of the lift. While there were no known instances of the latter occurring on either investigation, the movement of figures was widely reported in the first investigation. As this was not independently verified by video footage, no formal conclusions can be drawn.

The theatre is now fully reopen with a packed schedule of performances and we wish it well for its future success, regardless of the fact that this makes follow-up investigations more difficult!

INVESTIGATION OF THE CENTRAL FIRE STATION

18 August 2007 saw the first known paranormal investigation of a working fire station. It took place at the Central Fire Station in the heart of Swindon. PSI had begun, at that time, an initiative in co-operation with Swindon Borough Council entitled the *Haunted Swindon* project. A website was created to encourage the residents of Swindon to come forward and relate their paranormal experiences.

Background and Witness Interviews

Earlier in the year the PSI founders visited the district fire station at Stratton in Swindon as reports had come in, via the *Haunted Swindon* project website, of a range of strange and unexplained activity at the location. After the fire station staff interviews had been completed, it emerged that many of the accounts actually referred to the main fire station in central Swindon. This led the PSI founders to contact Wiltshire Fire Service with a request for an investigation.

During the preliminary investigation, one of PSI's founders conducted interviews with all the available witnesses. The client was made fully aware of the role that PSI could fulfil regarding unearthing the truth behind the alleged haunting. A full tour of the location was undertaken to ascertain the feasibility of conducting a full investigation.

Stories of the hauntings at the fire station date back at least 30 years. With this in mind, interviews took place with a number of fire station staff who gave their accounts of the unexplained events at the station.

During the initial interview stage, there were tales of doors being opened and closed, lights being turned on and off and footsteps being heard from the floor above, at the time when the dormitories were being redecorated and the mattresses were moved to the recreation area above. Another fireman in the middle floor bedroom reported he heard a 'party' going on upstairs, that almost sounded like a riot with furniture being thrown around. When he went up to ask them to stop, he found no one

Swindon's central fire station, set on the infamous Magic Roundabout.

was there and the rooms were just as they had been left. The sound of running footsteps had been heard by others and there have been many fleeting glimpses of figures. These figures included what was described as an old 'lock keeper' and apparent sightings of a 'drowned lady' walking up and down. In the dormitory, a shadowy figure had been seen at the foot of a bed, while the toilet where a figure had been seen and the canteen were noted as particularly haunted locations.

There is one story that was retold more than any of the others, which involved items of technical safety equipment. A distress signal unit (DSU) is used when a firefighter enters a smoke-filled building. Every member of the station personnel at the scene of the fire is issued with one of these vital pieces of equipment. Primarily, the DSU is designed to sound an alarm if a firefighter were to stop moving, thus signalling that person was in trouble or even possibly unconscious. One evening, not long after the watch change over, the firefighters on duty were shocked to discover all the alarms on the DSU's had been activated. This had never happened before and, in fact, has not happened since. The firemen were left shocked and confused by the incident, but what they found out in the following hours made many of them think there could have been an unusual explanation.

A firefighter from the previous watch was known to take the same route home after each shift and would often stop at a local sweet shop on his way. That night, however, as he stepped out of the shop he fell down, dying from a heart attack. At that exact moment, all the alarms at the fire station were activated. Some might say this was a coincidence, but others believe it was the spirit of the poor man saying his farewells.

History of the Station

The fire service in any town is an essential part of the community. Its role above all others is to serve the local population, saving untold numbers of lives and livelihoods through the quenching of the deadliest element: fire. As with any service of this nature, precise records and a well-documented history are kept, ensuring the search for background information on the location was somewhat easier for our team of researchers.

The Central Fire Station was built in the early 1960s and is located at the western corner of the junction between Drove Road and Fleming Way, in what is primarily a residential area of central Swindon. The 1889 Ordnance Survey map shows the site was mainly occupied by a large building known as Fairholm. Drove Road was the main route for the movement of cattle up the hill to the cattle markets in Swindon's Old Town. Swindon Wharf was also situated at what is now the north-west part of the site, adjacent to Fleming Way, but which was then part of the southern bank of the Wiltshire and Berkshire Canal. In the late 1920s and early 1930s a local resident recalls the site being known as Gillings Farm, and animals were regularly herded from there across Drove Road into open fields. At that time a music teacher, Madame Dockray, occupied a stone house on the site. Since then, the canal has disappeared to make way for the new housing estates at the location with all of the land flattened for development. More recent features added to the landscape of the area include the infamous Magic Roundabout, a system of five mini roundabouts merging as one.

PSI Investigates the Station

All information given in the form of witness testimony and historical findings was collated and, with this data, a plan for the investigation was drawn up by the PSI founders. None of the information was given to the remainder of the team before or during the investigation, so as not to prime the perceptions of the investigators.

In the early evening of 18 August 2007 the team assembled at the location and were greeted by the watch manager. The PSI founders gave a brief summary of the itinerary for the evening to ensure that the previously submitted plan was still acceptable. The team unpacked their equipment and set up the base room for the investigation briefing. The station personnel were happy to give us as much help (and space) as possible and they later retired to the canteen, which was not to be investigated at this time.

Following the briefing, the team were taken on a tour of the areas that were to be investigated, in order to point out any hazards or safety issues which might become apparent during the investigation. During this time the team also looked for any extraneous factors which could give anomalous results on the equipment. These factors were noted and included draughts, LED lights, luminous strips and so on.

Once all the necessary equipment for the investigation had been allocated, the team was split into two groups and the investigation began. PSI investigated bedroom one, the engine area, the first-floor corridor and the TV room. At the start of the investigation there were two teams of investigators but, for operational reasons, the teams had to merge for the final two sessions. This meant that meaningful comparisons of paranormal belief in relation to phenomena reporting could not be drawn.

All sessions lasted for 45 minutes and were followed by 15-minute breaks to refresh the team, replace full tapes and fit fresh batteries to any equipment that needed them. At the beginning, the middle and at the end of each session, a baseline test was conducted to give a set of readings measuring temperature, electromagnetic fields and negative ion fields, as well as exploratory photographs of the area. These would later be compared to the data collected during the investigation to highlight any anomalies. A further baseline test was conducted whenever participants reported experiences. Two séances took place and all investigators were asked to voice any perceived reactions.

Investigators' Experiences

Over the course of the evening, investigators experienced several auditory phenomena. This included clicks, taps and thuds. It must be kept in mind, however, that the location is a working fire station. While there were no call-outs for the firefighters during the night's research, and although all the firefighters were contained in one area, we must consider that these sounds were natural in origin. The new house effect is another possible explanation. This theory, as mentioned earlier, suggests that when somebody enters into a novel environment they identify sounds and noises that generally go unnoticed by people who know the environment well. As the team had never investigated this location before, it is entirely possible that they were identifying sounds which were natural to the building.

Bedroom One

Both teams investigated bedroom one at different times in the evening. There were numerous reports of activity in this room. At approximately 3sq m, it was a tight fit for the team. There was one large sliding window at the rear of the room, facing the entrance door, which was spring-loaded for closing, and a single bed was situated below the window running along the width of the room. The investigators made themselves as comfortable as possible in the circumstances and the following was reported:

All investigators heard someone walking in the corridor outside bedroom one. It was investigated but no one was found to be there.

One of the team felt that any person who had lain on the bed would experience the sensation that somebody's weight was on them, as if someone was leaning on them and crawling over them. Another investigator reported feeling that someone was watching her.

A noise was heard which sounded like a chair scraping outside the room, or perhaps upstairs, and the name Pete was perceived although no other person was present.

A team member felt that whoever occupied the room was re-enacting what they did in the past. The team member also sensed that the presence felt scared, as they did not understand why other people were sometimes in their room. A cold sensation was felt across two investigators' shoulders and all heard thudding noises from above or on the same level, as it was difficult to differentiate between the two. The team questioned if it could have been from the snooker table above or someone rocking on a chair.

One investigator related the feeling of a man having a heart attack. This could be the result of a coincidence since the account of the fireman who had a heart attack on the way home from the station, unknown to team members, coincided with unusual activity in the kit area and engine area rather than bedroom one.

Engine Area

The engine area was a vast garage containing five fire-engine appliances. A faint odour of oil could be smelt in the location and various draughts could be felt around the area. PVC curtains were hung between the engine room and the kit room, ensuring fast, efficient access to the appliances should the alarm bells sound. All this made the area a challenging proposition for a scientific study. Various experiences were felt in this location by both teams at differing times.

During an EVP session, a team member thought he heard a voice just after the question: 'Where do you come from?' was asked. The voice sounded like it said 'thank you', although it was very quiet. Movement was heard during the EVP session but it could have been from outside.

During the session, one investigator reported feeling a heavy atmosphere in the area and the whole team heard a clank from the far end of the area and another clank coming from where the first appliance was located. All investigators heard a clicking noise from the back of the area, and a coat that had been left on the floor appeared to have been moved.

The EMF meter readings at the first fire appliance were fluctuating between 0 and 2 (mG). The highest readings emanated from the tyres of one of the vehicles, but this was to be expected as the appliance was still warm, suggesting it had recently been driven. Also this appliance was newer than the others and, although we are not qualified to provide a conclusive answer, we agreed that due to its more modern nature this appliance might have more electronics on board, which would affect the level of EMF readings.

An investigator saw a clear figure walking at the front of the engine area. It is possible that this could have been one of the firemen on watch at the time, but it seems unlikely that they would have gone unnoticed. There was another account, some two minutes later, of a figure seen between the fire appliances. In addition, a whisper was heard in the engine area, but this could have been accounted for by wind underneath the many external doors.

The engine area, or appliance bay, has reports dating back decades.

The muster room.

First-Floor Corridor

The most compelling incident of the study was towards the end of the session on the dormitory floor. As the group was spaced evenly along the corridor, several investigators thought they heard voices coming from the gym. Upon entering the room, investigators saw the rear door, leading to the stairwell, slowly closing. Rushing out through the door, the group were unable to identify anyone within the vicinity. Trying to recreate the situation, it was deemed that someone would have to have been moving at an incredible rate to go through the gym door and make it to the bottom of the stairs unseen and, indeed, unheard.

While standing near the pole drop door, one of the investigators heard voices through the door. Although fire personnel were on site, they were not in the vicinity at the time. Then the same team member felt that someone was tickling the bottom of their back during the EVP session. Also, the footsteps of someone climbing the stairs at the end of the corridor could be clearly heard by one team member who was nearby, but there was nobody in sight.

TV Room

This is probably the most comfortable room the PSI have ever investigated. This is where the firefighters spend their downtime, relaxing on soft furnishings while watching the television. Unfortunately for the team, this was also potentially the noisiest room we would encounter on this investigation. A long tall window gave us a perfect view of the busy Magic Roundabout, but with the view came the traffic noise.

Two of the team thought they heard a dragging noise from the corridor. This could have been traffic noise from outside, but it did sound as if it was emanating from within the corridor, rather than the outside. Another possible explanation was the shower room, which has an automatic flush on the urinal. This could account for the noise heard but cannot be proven at this time.

Psychic Impression

During the investigation, many experiences were reported, not all of which had a rational explanation. Glimpses of figures, doors closing and the repeated noises heard throughout the night added to an enjoyable and rewarding investigation for the whole team.

Various pieces of information were provided by the team during the investigation, such as the perceived name of Pete, the sensations felt in bedroom one of someone crawling over a body in the bed, and also the feeling of confusion and threat by the presence of people in what was 'his' room. The sensation of being tickled on the lower back, while in the television room, was also an interesting occurrence.

The gym door, which unaccountably opened.

Analysing the Evidence

The investigation generated 169 photographs and over eight hours of video footage for analysis. Three units of video camera evidence and 40 photographs, all digital, withstood the first stage of analysis. Three experienced analysts conducted the second stage of analysis, which 31 photographs withstood. After ruling out examples of human error, equipment, reflection, dust and known light source, only one photo withstood the second strand of analysis.

The photograph shows a participant facing away from the camera with an unusual red light over her hair. This participant was using the EMF meter, which was out of shot at the time the photograph was taken. The photo suffered from a long exposure; the shutter speed was a half second rather than one thirtieth of a second, which represents the norm. This dragging of light from the EMF meter likely took place because the position of the meter was moved over this half second.

There were reports made by investigators of seeing moving shadows and changes in darkness. As the fire station is situated on a busy roundabout this could be caused by car headlights. Additionally, during an EVP session one member thought they heard a voice saying 'thank you'.

Several pieces of equipment did malfunction over the course of the night. During an EVP session the compact disc player skipped straight to track 11 when selecting track nine and the batteries

The corridor outside the firefighters' dormitories.

drained halfway through on the dictaphone. Tapes mysteriously ended before reaching capacity. There was also one report of a battery on a video camera, which had been charged and checked before the investigation, having drained during the session. These were rare occurrences, although nothing unusual was captured on film.

Conclusion

During the investigation, 14 participants reported 87 subjective experiences in a little over three hours of field time.

The reports of fleeting figures and the movement of the coat were indeed of interest but no physical evidence was captured on any of the equipment deployed in these areas. Investigator tiredness and optical illusions caused by traffic headlights cannot be ruled out as rational explanations. The numerous reports of thuds, clicking and taps can be explained purely as the cooling of the building and the new house effect.

After analysis, two-thirds of these experiences were categorised as subjective experiences. All experiences that were not verified were ruled out as evidence. Two cases, one of figures seen in the engine area and one of specific EVP, remain of interest. 30 per cent of the experiences were categorised as subjective-verified. However, potential natural explanations could account for these experiences. The incident of a door appearing to be closed in the gym area remains of interest. The small number of other incidents appeared to fall into the category of whole-real experience. Compelling natural explanations could be put forward for those.

Environmental conditions were consistently monitored throughout the investigation but were recognised as being necessarily flawed. Nine significant fluctuations occurred. Some were immediately explainable and none coincided with any other phenomena so they were likely to be chance occurrences.

At this time PSI are unable to confirm whether Central Fire Station is actually haunted or not, therefore the case remains open and no formal conclusion can be drawn. Various aspects of the evidence remain interesting and the case would benefit from further research to shed light on the findings.

INVESTIGATION OF STANTON PARK FARMHOUSE

Background and Eyewitness Interviews

'You must have heard about the haunted house down in the woods at Stanton Park?' enquired a friend one evening in the pub. The house to which they were referring was Stanton Park Farmhouse and rumours suggested that the house was haunted by a woman who had been seen to appear at the house's window. A search on the Internet unearthed a forum posting from a young male who had admitted to trespassing at the property when it was abandoned, and had reported his strange experiences when at the site. Crashes, bangs and thuds reverberated through the building and barn. Icy cold spots were felt. His belongings would mysteriously move from part of the building to another. Outlines of figures had also been seen.

Curious about the site, I mentioned it to a colleague over coffee at work the next day and her reaction solidified the PSI's need to investigate the house. She had been part of the team that had been responsible for renovating the site and she, too, had heard the rumours that it was haunted. The feeling of being watched and a strong sense of presence were her offerings in cementing its haunted reputation.

When we approached the Swindon Ranger Team, who now occupy the site, they were unaware of the tales associated with the buildings and had nothing to report themselves, but were exceptionally co-operative and granted us full access to the complex.

History of the Site

Stanton Park Farmhouse lies beside the lake in Stanton Country Park, to the south of a village called Stanton Fitzwarren. This village is approximately two miles south-west of Highworth and is deceptively adjacent to the urban mass of Swindon. The village place name means 'the settlement by the stone, belonging to the family of Fitzwarren'. In 1086 the Domesday Book gives the manor

The lake of Stanton Park, adjacent to the farmhouse.

The farmhouse was uninhabited for some years.

of Stanton as owned by Grimbald Goldsmith. The Parish Church of St Leonard is approximately 500m north of the site and is Norman in origin. In the 12th century, the manor was split between the Fitzherbert and Fitzwarren families, the latter possessing the settlement that now bears its name and includes the site. Around 1650 the manor passed to the Hippisley family, who kept it until 1929. In the mid-18th century the estate included gardens, an orchard, woodland and a deer park. In 1804 the original mediaeval manorial estate was inherited by Revd J. Ashfordbury-Trenchard (via his mother, a Hippisley heiress). He found much of the village in a ruinous condition and devoted a good deal of expense to its renovation. As part of this project he developed a large area as landscaped parkland, including features such as a lake, a folly, and ornamental trees. The farmhouse (which is the main building on the site) was built shortly after 1820 and is surrounded to the south and west by a stream that feeds the man-made lake to the north (this lake was originally simply a boggy depression with a stream).

Although poor data collection by successive census enumerators prohibits clear evidence for habitation of the site, the 1881 census does list Park Farm, which was then occupied by the Clark family: Charles Clark (aged 57, a shepherd, born at Horsham, Sussex), his wife Fanny (53, born in Wiltshire), a son William (16, agricultural labourer, born in Stanton Fitzwarren) and daughters Elizabeth (14, scholar, born in Stanton Fitzwarren) and Mary (9, scholar, born in Highworth).

In 1996 Swindon Borough Council purchased 74 hectares (185 acres) of the parkland from Tom Charnock (former Bluebird Toys executive). The area included the lake, meadows and woodland, as well as the site. Now known as Stanton Park, the land was opened to the public in 2000. By this time, Stanton Park Farmhouse and its outbuildings had fallen into disrepair. A local community group, Parks DIY, began tackling this problem in the spring of 2005 and students from Swindon College were also involved in the restoration work, which aimed to convert the dilapidated house and barns into an environmental education and visitor centre.

Almost immediately to the south-west of the site lies the Great Wood, which is classified as 'ancient semi-natural woodland', indicating it has been standing for at least 400 years, and has experienced limited woodland management.

PSI Investigates

On the evening of 15 September 2007 the PSI team arrived to begin the investigation. The team began by taking baseline readings throughout the site and by 8.45pm were ready to begin a séance in the first-floor office.

First séance

During this initial séance the atmosphere was reported by various team members as feeling 'heavy' and 'oppressive'. Investigators reported perceiving the room's natural light levels to fluctuate, becoming lighter or darker, despite no man-made light sources being present. The sound of a woman humming, happy in her work, was reported by one team member, while another member felt they heard the distant sound of two men having a conversation – likening it to a radio being left on in the distance. The clock in the room was also reported as only ticking intermittently, but further investigation showed that it was not ticking when the hour and minute hands were passing over one another and this sound was natural in nature.

It was during this séance that one investigator perceived the presence of a woman, aged in her late 40s, of slim build, with a ruddy complexion, long brown hair, dirty face and resembling a typical farm-wife. The investigator felt that her name was Eliza or Elisa and that she had once lived in the older part of building.

At the end of this session the team split into two groups and the investigation began in earnest. Over the course of the following hours, the two groups spent time in the barn, the mushroom room (so-called by the founders of the team after they discovered mushrooms growing in the room during their preliminary visit, in the unoccupied part of the building) and the first and second-floor offices.

Still photographs were taken at regular intervals in all the areas being investigated and video cameras recorded the scene during each session, as well as being used in areas without team personnel as lock-offs. Baseline equipment readings were taken every 15 minutes throughout the night and EVP experiments were conducted in each session in rotating conditions.

The Barn

In the barn, members reported the smell of haylage and coal-tar smoke. Some felt the temperature drop noticeably and felt as if something was right in front of them. All heard knocking or tapping sounds and, during the first EVP experiment, all heard what sounded like someone walking across the rafters. The sound of music in the distance was reported, as well as the sound of close, heavy breathing. One investigator sensed the faint presence of a tall, thin male and the presence of a young boy kneeling, rocking and sobbing, as if there had been some kind of accident. The team member felt that the boy was about 17 years old and was wearing a white shirt and dark trousers, dressed like a farm-hand. Shuffling noises were also heard and a bright flash of white light was seen.

The Mushroom Room

This room was reported by investigators as feeling progressively 'thicker', 'heavier' and 'darker' over the course of the night. One investigator claims to have seen a gathering red mass in the middle

The former farmhouse's barn was the site of various 'experiences' during PSI's investigations.

of the room which was, to her, synonymous with death. The sensation of somebody walking behind the group was reported by one investigator and several cold spots were felt by team members, but not corroborated by temperature readings.

First-Floor Office
Several thumps were heard and reports of shifting volumes of light were also made in the first-floor office. The sound of voices was heard (but not captured) and a flash of light was seen to make its way across the office door.

Second-Floor Office
There was one account made of an investigator seeing the movement of red and green lights in this room, but this was solved by identifying the room's motion sensors as flicking between red and green. No other reports were made in this area, nor was any footage of interest captured.

The Team Returns
Due to the amount of reports made by investigators, the team sought permission to revisit the site a few months later, in December 2007, to continue their study of the building. We will consider all reports and footage together. The format of this second investigation mirrored that of the first, for the sake of research validity and, again, saw the team split into two groups to study the four identified areas.

Séances
Both séances were held in the mushroom room and, during the initial séance, investigators reported hearing footsteps, having tingling sensations in their heads, seeing a pulsating 'darkness', feeling as though they were swaying and seeing pinpricks of red light. The investigator who had picked up on a lady called Elisa/Eliza in the first investigation also felt her presence during this session, but queried whether her name was actually Eva. This investigator also felt that the room would have once been papered in dark green and that there would have been a double bed in the room that was made up with dark red blankets and sheets.

The First-Floor Office
One investigator reported seeing a figure standing by the door, but upon investigation, this was found to be caused by a heavy coat hanging on the back of the door. Clicks were heard during sessions in this room and flashes of light were also seen. One team member reported feeling very emotional and sad after spending time in this room.

The Second-Floor Office
The only report made in the top floor office on this return visit was the perception of a dark, moving mass.

The Barn
The sound of shuffling was detected by several investigators and everyone experienced an increasing coldness. Flashes of light were also reported and one investigator said they felt very edgy and nervous in the barn.

The Mushroom Room

Considerably less activity was reported in the mushroom room during the team's return visit, but incidences of note included seeing flashes of light and the perception of somebody standing in the doorway.

Analysing the evidence

The various reports of humming or music being heard during the investigations have possible origin in the neighbouring hotel or, perhaps, the radios of passing cars. The sounds of voices could possibly have come from people in the woods. Although the park is officially closed after dusk, it is still accessible by foot and a dog walker was seen by two team members. On clear, still nights, such as the nights that both investigations were held, sound does carry very easily.

The sound of somebody walking on the rafters of the barn was possibly caused by a breeze or perhaps by vermin. Mice or rats may also be the culprits in regard to the shuffling sounds reported in this area due to the exposed nature of the building. Investigators also reported the occasional smell of haylage in the barn and the smell of smoke. Experience from prior investigations has revealed that smells related to a building's prior use – across the short, medium and longer term – can linger upon its fabric for an undetermined length of time. It is also possible that external smells may have been carried on the wind, infiltrating the building.

The flashes of light and light movement which were reported by all investigators, across both teams and throughout both investigations, were identified as being caused by the opposing team's camera flashes and torches and, during the latter investigation, fireworks.

There were several reports of clicks, knocks and thumps made at both nights spent at the farmhouse. Potential causes include retraction and settling of the building or its contents, unintentional movement of investigators and noise from electrical or mechanical equipment, including camcorders and heating systems.

The increasing sense of coldness in the barn during the second investigation was corroborated by equipment readings, and thermometers confirmed that, by the end of the night, the ground temperature was down to minus four degrees Celsius, with investigators' cars having a hefty layer of ice on their windscreens!

The reported perception of the presence of a woman in her late 40s, named Eliza, Elisa or Eva, may be of interest as the 1881 census lists an Elizabeth Clark residing at Farm Park, although at the time she was aged 14. However, as has been noted in the site history, census records relating to the site are not as detailed as would have been hoped. Similarly, as previously stated, historical data is not exhaustive. In regard to the presence of a young male in the barn, there are no known accounts of an accident having occurred in there but farms can be dangerous places and, as HSE records do not go back that far, we are unable to shed any further light on that perception.

The mushroom room proved to be one of the most interesting rooms over the course of both investigations, with many reports being made by investigators but none being corroborated by video footage. It is of great interest that this room, which was perceived by investigators as the 'most spooky', with their perception being recorded after only 10 seconds of exposure through context questionnaires, elicited the greatest number of reports by team members over both investigations. The room is, by far, the darkest (as illustrated through lux readings) and most dilapidated of all areas investigated and this may have increased investigators' sense of vulnerability and did, to some extent, reflect the traditional haunted house as portrayed by the media. The context of this room would have contributed towards investigators' reported perceptions and, as a result of the context questionnaires, investigators may have felt under pressure to justify their independent ranking of the room by making more reports in this room than in other areas being studied.

With the exception of psychological reports (e.g. feeling oppressive atmospheres), all other accounts made in the mushroom room have been explained. The moving volumes of light were probably caused by the security light outside coming on and off intermittently, or by the other team's cameras and torches, or the nearby fireworks. The investigator who experienced the swaying sensation was suffering from an ear infection at the time of the investigation and this may have affected his balance. The red lights that were seen are thought to have come from the infra-red booster beam that was attached to the video cameras recording the room, and the cold spots were likely to be caused by draughts coming in through gaps in the window-frame.

None of the photographic evidence taken at the site appeared to contain significant images, with anomalies being ruled out as being caused by dust, reflection and other pieces of equipment or human error.

With regards to the video footage, on two occasions, within a 40-second spell, a knocking sound could be heard on the video footage. On a further occasion within the time-span, two participants reported the auditory perception of a thump from outside the office door in the stairwell area. While it may be tempting to link all three events, such speculation is purely tentative in the absence of more revealing evidence. It should be noted that a feature of many hand-held video recorders is the auto-gain circuit. Its purpose is to sustain a consistent audio volume across the length of any recording. Quiet noises, which may not attract the attention of a listener, become magnified and their worth, as evidence, is reduced. Common causes of thumps, knocks and clicks magnified by the auto-gain circuit typically include accidental investigator movement, retraction of floors, fixtures and fittings, and radiators and electronic equipment.

There were no anomalous equipment readings for which explanations could not be found.

Conclusion

The case of Stanton Park Farmhouse is of great fascination to the team as, although there are relatively few prior accounts of activity at the site, investigators persist in having unverifiable experiences. There is no objective evidence, however, to suggest that the site is in any way haunted. The farmhouse, however, conveniently and quite neatly, fits the common perception of what a haunted house should look like. Are its mere appearance and dereliction feeding the imaginations of trained, rational and scientific investigators?

With cameras and equipment failing to shed any light on the reported phenomena, the team look forward to spending more time at the site in the future in an attempt to uncover the cause of the reports being made.

Investigation of the Planks Auction Rooms, Old Town

Situated adjacent to Lawn Woods and the former Goddard family estate, the site of the Planks Auction Rooms has had several tales of hauntings reported.

One night the two auction room workers drove into the yard with a consignment of goods for auction. They had keys to the alarm system and gates, and were going to leave the van overnight for unloading in the morning. Loud crashing sounds coming from inside the old building alerted them to what sounded like vandalism in the store-room. They removed the padlock from the main door and ventured inside, and were surprised to find it perfectly calm, with all its antiques and other contents intact and in order. They left, re-securing the door, and were shocked to hear the loud banging sounds start over again. Suspecting there were still intruders in the building, they called the police. Five officers responded and duly witnessed the sounds of a commotion; one officer also saw a face in an upstairs window. Upon entering the premises they found everything was peaceful and in its place and, despite a thorough search that included the upstairs offices, neither trespassers nor any other source of the noises was found. Baffled, they exited and locked up again. When the noises promptly resumed, the police judged that they were unable to assist further and departed. The workmen similarly decided against another sortie into what they now felt was a haunted place, and left. Upon leaving, one of the police officers confided in the auction room workers that, upon arrival, he had seen a face gazing down at him from one of the upstairs windows.

In the week before the team were due to investigate the case, a work colleague of one of the group's founders reported that she had once worked at the site in the late 1980s and said that the buildings were well-known among staff to be haunted. Noises had been heard coming from the first floor, when no one was known to be there. Few staff would enter the first floor alone due to the intense sense of presence and feelings of deep discomfort in the area. There were rumours that the spirit of a child haunted that floor and that a face had been seen at the window. Additionally, one of the outbuildings had been boarded up and was never used, but nobody seemed to know why.

The site has been unoccupied for a number of years and it is due for redevelopment. The group was successful in identifying the developer and agency that had taken ownership of the complex, and they kindly granted the team access to conduct research into the reported phenomena.

History of the Site

Until recently, an auction house popularly known as the Planks occupied the site. The premises are situated in the Old Town district of Swindon, and were erected as a stable and coach-house serving the Goddard family home, probably in the 18th century.

The complex consists of a two-storey building constructed of coursed limestone rubble, under a half-hipped tiled mansard roof accommodating an attic floor, with several outbuildings adjacent to the main building, including a recently built concrete room with a corrugated roof.

The Domesday Book records that in 1086 that the site was in the hands of Odin the Chamberlain, and the area later became part of the manor of High Swindon. The manor passed back into the king's possession, and Henry III granted it to William de Valence, Earl of Pembroke. In the 1560s the Manor of Swindon (which included the area formerly known as High Swindon) was purchased by Thomas Goddard. The manor house was situated within approximately 100m of the

The Planks was part of the Goddard Estate and later an auction house.

site and was replaced on the same site by a substantial house called Swindon House in around 1770. It is this phase of building that most likely saw the erection of the stable and coach-house that is the now the Planks.

Swindon House was renamed the Lawn in the mid-19th century and the Goddard family remained lords of the manor until the death of Major Fitzroy Pleydell Goddard in 1927. The Lawn remained home to his widow Eugenia Kathleen until 1931.

During World War Two, the Lawn was occupied by British and US forces and was significantly damaged by the latter. In 1947 the estate was bought by Swindon Corporation. Falling further into dereliction, the Lawn was demolished in 1952 while the grounds were opened to the public as a park. The Planks was purchased privately and opened as an auction house that served generations of local people. In 1970 the building was awarded Grade II listed status. The Planks auction house closed in January 2003, having been run by Bristol Auction Rooms for more than 20 years.

The adjacent Goddard estate was large and numerous hauntings are associated with it, and those found to be in the immediate vicinity are also affected. It is probable that a location identified on a forum as the Manor, and located vaguely but in the immediate vicinity of the site, actually refers to the Lawn, seat of the lords of the manor. The writer notes that a 'grey lady' haunted the premises and adds that one of the female staff not only heard footsteps upstairs when nobody was there, but also reported that the strong scent of lavender was always present in one of the rooms.

PSI Investigates

On the night of 10 November 2007 the PSI team undertook a night of study at the site to try and attempt to uncover what may have been the cause of, or contributed towards the perception of, the reported haunting.

As the site had been unoccupied for such a long time, the team were courteous in informing nearby residents that they were going to be in attendance at the site. They also reinforced their relationship with Wiltshire Police by logging their visit with the constabulary, to circumvent any impromptu visits from officers if there were reports of unusual activity occurring at the normally unoccupied site.

The team were mildly hampered by the fact that the building had been out of use for the previous four years and as such had no running water, bathroom facilities or electricity. The team had rarely worked under such conditions in the past, therefore the hospitality of a nearby public house was greatly appreciated by the group when nature called! Gas-powered lamps in the concrete outbuilding provided some much appreciated light and warmth for the team during break times and flasks of coffee were rapidly consumed.

The team were randomly pre-assigned into two groups and this was the first investigation for new investigators who had recently undergone the intense PSI recruitment period – consisting of an induction evening, application form, interview, training weekend and, now, peer-assessed fieldwork. Given the conditions in which the team was to be working, it was something of a baptism of fire.

Over the course of several hours, the investigators participated in two séances, the study of four identified areas of interest, EVP experiments and frequent baseline checks using the team's armoury of visual, auditory and environmental monitoring equipment. Visual instrumental transcommunication experiments were not possible at the site due to the lack of power available and the prohibitive cost of hiring generators or similar.

Investigators' experiences and analysis of experiences
The four areas that were identified as being worthy of study were the main auction room, the first room of the first floor, the courtyard and the abandoned outbuilding.

Auction Room

During the sessions in the main auction room, four investigators sensed the presence of a man in the area and one investigator felt this presence to be following the group throughout the entirety of the investigation. These same investigators made several reports of feeling the man to be stood near to each of them at various points. The investigators reported these sensations in front of one another, so it is possible that they influenced one another in their reports. No video or camera footage taken depicted the man that they reported.

'Dancing' pinpricks of white light were seen to be moving around one part of the room by one investigator. As this report was subjective, not verified by other investigators, nor captured on camera, it is possible that the light was physiological in nature and caused by the investigator's eyes adjusting to low light conditions. Additionally, however, a small ball of white light was reported to have been moving from one side of the group to the other by one investigator but, again, this was not verified by others nor captured on camera.

There were two instances of equipment malfunction during the time spent in this area. The first was of a rapid battery drain in one investigator's camera. Due to the fact that the area was relatively exposed to the elements and with the naturally falling temperatures (note that this investigation was conducted in November), it is thought that the low temperature may have contributed towards this draining effect; this is supported by research that has illustrated the adverse effect of low temperatures on household batteries. The second malfunction was reported when a voice was heard to emanate from an investigator's pocket – the dictaphone had seemingly replayed the last recorded track. Upon examination, the dictaphone had not been put into the 'hold' condition and, as a result, its movement within the investigator's pocket could have easily led to the 'play' button being depressed.

Several 'popping' sounds and bangs were reported by team members and captured on camera. These coincided with flashes of light also being reported. Due to the investigation's proximity to 5 November, and supported by the investigators' venture outside, fireworks were identified as being the most likely cause.

Movement was heard by an investigator in the adjacent courtyard but, upon examination, no natural cause was easily identifiable. However, foxes are known to frequent the area, as reinforced by old track marks found in the mud. Male voices were also heard coming from outside but these were found to be natural in origin and were caused by two men walking along the nearby road.

A bluey-green light was seen by several investigators to glow on one of the auction room's walls, but this was a result of one of the video cameras' LCD displays having not been shut. Several 'swoops' of white light were reported by investigators to cross across the rear wall and, initially, this proved to be of great interest to the team due to the repeatability of the phenomena and no immediate cause being identified. However, when two investigators moved into the courtyard to analyse the effect further, they were able to confirm that the other group's torch beams in the outbuilding opposite was the cause. Due to the age of the buildings and their general disrepair, it was proven that light from the beams could penetrate gaps in the brickwork of the auction room to create the reported effects.

First-Floor Office

One experiencer reported a sinister change of atmosphere during the time spent in this area. This was accompanied by them sensing a presence, perceiving the room to become darker and feeling 'heavier'. In addition, the member also reported feeling dizzy and that their head was 'spinning'. It must be recognised that, as the eyewitness interviewer, this investigator knew the history of the site and the previously reported accounts of phenomena. This investigator had also ranked the room as being the 'most spooky' of all areas under investigation and these factors must be considered as contributing towards their experience. The sensation of dizziness may have been a result of the floorboards in this floor being uneven and prone to slight movement.

There were, however, several incidences reported in this area for which the team currently cannot conclusively account. Clicking sounds, a pale green light, the sound of metallic banging, a growling sound and a door which had previously been closed, but was then found to be open, were among the instances reported by investigators. The clicking sounds may have been caused by the floor resettling, as the building had not been used for a considerable time, and the sudden weight of the team may have contributed towards these sounds. Due to the general disrepair of the site, no guarantees can be made in regard to the robustness of the door latches and hinges, and this may have resulted in the door being found open, although left shut. The metallic banging did not seem to imitate the sound of fireworks heard previously in the evening, but this, as a possibility, must be considered. The pale green light was only seen by one investigator and due to the subjective nature of the report it is impossible to draw any firm conclusions. The reported sound of growling was heard by all investigators present at the time and occurred during an EVP session. Despite the additional sound recorders being used at the time, the noise was not captured on sound recorder or video camera and its cause and origin remains a mystery.

Outbuilding

There were two psychic impressions picked up by investigators in opposing teams during time spent in the outbuilding. An investigator from the first team reported that they felt that a man had either been hung in the outbuilding, or had hung himself in there. The other investigator's report was of sensing much happier times – the perception of a young man and woman coming to the outbuilding to enjoy one another while hiding their affair from their respective partners. This investigator connected the names Darryl, Pearce and Jones to the images they perceived.

Several clicks and taps were heard during sessions in this area, but dripping rainwater was identified as being the cause. Shuffling sounds and non-specific movement sounds were reported as coming from the room adjacent to the outbuilding but, while no obvious cause could be found, vermin are known to frequent the site and could have contributed towards these sounds.

Investigators from both teams reported seeing what they perceived to be a figure standing in the doorway to the outbuilding, always described as being around 5ft 8in in height and moving from side to side. The buddleia bush, which obscures part of the doorway and naturally sways in the breeze, was thought to be the most likely explanation for these reports.

There was one interesting incident that did occur in the outbuilding but does not specifically relate to it. Two investigators, in the same team, concurrently reported that they thought that a named investigator from the other team was about to enter the room and say 'hello everyone'! There would have been no known reason for these investigators to think that this would happen – as it had never happened before nor would there be any reason for it to ever happen – and the team are certain that it was not a hoax set up between the two investigators. What makes this incident all the more interesting is that there was another case of what seemed to be specific ESP occurring between these two investigators at another investigation which, again, did not relate to the venue being investigated. This apparent phenomenon involving these individuals may form part of the group's future research into extra-sensory perception.

Courtyard

Although there have been no known reports of activity in the courtyard, it was placed under study due to reports of a face being seen at an upstairs window, gazing out. The investigators were not told what they were looking for when studying this area.

There were, again, two psychic impressions made by team members in this area. The first was that the investigator perceived that this would have once been a busy thoroughfare with horses galloping by. The second report was of sensing that there was once a fire at the site and a woman was stood at one of the first-floor windows crying out for help. The investigator that reported this sensation was not aware that there had been previous reports of an indistinguishable face looking out of a first-floor window.

The only other report made by team members in this area was the perception that there was general, but unspecific, movement being seen in one of the windows. It is possible, however, that this may have been caused by the movement of trees in the breeze reflecting upon the window-pane.

Analysing the Footage

Over the course of the investigation, over 100 photographs were taken but none survived second-stage analysis. At second-stage analysis, all anomalies captured were identified as being caused by dust particles, reflection, human error or known light sources.

Two units of video footage reached the second stage. The first one depicted the 'swoop' of white light that had been reported by investigators and was identified as being caused by torchlight. The second unit was auditory in nature and sounded like a small object bouncing across a hard surface. This sound was not acknowledged or reported by investigators at the time and is possibly a result of the video camera's auto-gain circuit, as discussed in other chapters.

There were no anomalous environmental readings collected over the course of the investigation.

Conclusion

Despite the somewhat adverse conditions, the team audited and monitored the site thoroughly over the course of the investigation. Many of their experiences were natural in origin, as we have illustrated in this chapter, but are we any closer to solving the historic reports which initiated this investigation?

The answer, quite simply, is no. Rarely, if ever, are we able to draw firm conclusions from an isolated site visit. In fact, even in the cases into which we have conducted longitudinal research, we are seldom able to fully explain the phenomena reported. Historic accounts with no available first-hand eyewitnesses are a hugely hampering factor when conducting research into hauntings. Even when such witnesses are available, however, the likelihood of their reported phenomena reoccurring while the team is in the situation is remote. Our presence at a site may allow us to identify natural aspects that may have contributed towards someone's experience but, without the incident reoccurring in our presence, it is impossible to provide firm conclusions.

INVESTIGATION OF OLIVE HOUSE, OLD TOWN

As a result of promotional work for the *Haunted Swindon* project, the team were contacted by two social workers who had formerly worked at Olive House and had had experiences that they wanted to share. Interviews ensued and current staff members' many first-hand and secondary accounts were gathered. There had been rumours that a child had been locked in the sky room on the top

The former council offices at Olive House.

floor when it had been a children's home and this was accompanied by reports of her being seen, as a ghost, both in the room itself and looking up at the window from the outside. Another child was also rumoured to have been locked in a cupboard under the stairs and sightings of her were also retold. One of the social workers recounted her experience of having seen a woman wearing a long dark dress cross the toilet corridor. Plump and aged 40–50 years old, she was said to resemble the photograph of a woman on the wall in the entrance porch. There were also accounts of items disappearing to then reappear somewhere entirely different, and other reports claiming a strong sense of presence in the toilet corridor and first floor.

History

Olive House is situated in the original Swindon at the top of Kingshill – an area that does have a long history and is also of archaeological interest, with remnants of Roman and Saxon periods found. It has been continually inhabited since prehistoric times. The building was built in the late 19th century and is a large villa-style detached property. It has been a private residence for most of its history. For a number of years, the house has been owned by Swindon Borough Council and was home to the Child Health Team, part of the Social Services department. In 1990 it was included in the Prospect Place Conservation Designated area. Today, however, it has been sold with an unknown future.

Paranormal activity reports of any phenomena are not readily available. As an interesting footnote, however, there has been a recent sighting of a UFO in the nearby area of Eastcott Hill. This may have no connection, but reports of UFO sightings and hauntings have been connected in the past.

The decision to investigate was decided as part of the *Haunted Swindon* project. The added incentive was the time-limit, as it was to be sold to developers by the end of 2007.

The Preliminary Investigation

This was conducted by the founders of PSI. The objective was to establish witness evidence, to find out any health and safety problems and make sure there was nothing on site that could affect the team, to have a plan of the site, and conduct checks to establish natural sounds, temperature, air pressure, electromagnetic fields and any other normal environmental factors. The rooms that were planned to be investigated were also photographed. One founder member interviewed the witnesses and recorded information onto a digital recorder, so an accurate record could be made of what they reported.

Investigation

On 27 July 2007 the PSI team arrived at Olive House for the investigation. The equipment used during this investigation included two-way radios for communication, two CD players for electronic voice phenomena (EVP) experiments, and a wide range of environmental, auditory and visual monitoring equipment.

PSI focused on specific rooms as they represented locations of reported activity. The planned agenda consisted of two teams and their set locations to investigate. Each team member had also been allocated their own tasks. Before commencing, there was a briefing and a welcome outlining the health and safety issues. Everybody signed a disclaimer form that also registered those that were present. The equipment was handed out to the team and checked to ensure working order, cameras and watches were synchronised and equipment was, where possible, calibrated. Several forms were filled in, including Thalbourne's belief scale, 'your feelings at the moment' scale and a contexting form that aims to measure how haunted (or not) one subjectively feels each area may be. The investigators were then divided into two teams to commence the investigation of Olive House.

To make sure everything ran safely and smoothly, one last important and familiar task was completed. This involved visiting all areas under study and carrying out an extraneous factors audit. This was to identify any natural or present factors that could hamper or mislead what the teams might see, hear or even smell. This includes exit signs that give off a glow and standby lights that sometimes flash on and off.

The whole team held a séance at the start of the evening. Usually a male and female voice are used to see if any initial contact is going to be made by anything that may be present. A digital voice recorder was used for any team member to report their experiences, to be used for future reference. The séance was also recorded by a video camera that was placed to view the whole scene.

The team then moved into their two groups, each with its planned agenda. Each team had a member that carried a two-way radio so as to ensure constant communication between them. At the beginning, middle and end of each session, the baseline tests were conducted. These consisted of electromagnetic field meter readings, spot temperature readings, negative ion detector readings and photographs. A data logger was elevated on a tripod by each team and this recorded temperature and humidity every 10 seconds. This information was then downloaded onto a computer at the end of the investigation.

Experiments

Each team set up kinetic lock-off experiments in the areas being investigated. A lock-off consists of a piece of paper and a trigger object. This is placed on the paper and carefully drawn around and two motion detectors are placed on either side. Digital photographs are taken and at least one video camera is placed to view the whole scene – to make sure that if the object did move it could be seen whether any human intervention gave it a helping hand. However, there is a possibility that unseen natural forces, such as vibration, could act on the object.

In electronic voice phenomena experiments, a CD player and a digital voice recorder are put about 12in apart. The experiment consists of two two-minute segments. During each one, baseline photographs are taken and the scene also recorded by a video camera. This experiment was set in place at Olive House and the recorder was turned on and, in the first two minutes, the participants remained silent, acting as the control segment. In the second two minutes they asked a set of questions divided equally between male and female voices, with a 20-second interval to allow for possible responses. The CD player in this experiment was used in several different conditions. In the first two minutes it was the control condition, where the CD player is turned on, but not playing a track. This was followed by a white noise track, followed by brown noise in the next session and in the last session pink noise. The different sound conditions were chosen in advance by the team leader.

In instrumental transcommunication (ITC), a television was put on with no input signal. A video camera was placed 24in away. It was connected to the TV from its own video out socket and to the TV from its own video in socket. The camera zoom was set to recommended guidelines and was then switched on for just 10 seconds. This experiment was predominantly conducted to see whether any images or faces emerged.

In Ganzfeld experiments, a willing volunteer is sat on a chair and the proceedings are explained to them. This is an extra-sensory perception experiment often used in parapsychology laboratories.

The participant has headphones put on and they listen to white noise. Their vision is impaired and a red light is switched on. A voice recorder is also switched on and put near to the person. The participant is then asked to vocalise any thoughts, feelings or visions before they are debriefed and their experiences are discussed. The theory is that, under these conditions, they are more likely to experience ESP, introspection and hallucinations. Careful consideration was made of the ethics of this approach before incorporating it into the investigation, and safeguards were put in place.

Investigation Design

Design is important and provides an explanation and precise reasons as to why we investigate in the way we do, along with the implications of these techniques. The purpose of a paranormal investigation is to try and record incidences in an objective manner and to gather scientific evidence of anomalies and phenomena. It is essential that we use a tailored and robust methodology. The use of random equipment may give personal proof, but will be unlikely to convince anyone else. Similarly, if an investigation report poses more questions than answers it can be of little use to the research fraternity. PSI investigations have a stated design, which is strictly adhered to, and the investigators are well-trained and disciplined. A clear methodological technique provides an essential basis for evidential analysis.

Eyewitness Testimony

During the investigation, the investigator acted as a participant and was instructed to record experimental events and their own thoughts, including feelings and unusual activity detected by their senses. On this and each research investigation the teams were not given any information on the site which they were visiting, so that no ideas could be established in their minds that could influence what they perceived to see, feel or hear. Apart from the eyewitness interviews, the team went in with an open mind and no prior knowledge. In certain locations, such as museums, this may not always be possible, so it is then up to the individual not to read any exposed information. There is, however, the possibility that the very action of participation on an investigation can stimulate a team member to expect activity, thus creating imaginary thoughts, sounds and images. Sometimes it can cause other members to experience similar phenomena.

Investigation Results

Top Gallery and Sky Room

During the session held in this area, batteries from a digital camera, which had been fully charged, drained within moments of starting. A steady hum was heard to come from downstairs, which one investigator perceived to be a moaning sound. A white flash of light coming from the stairwell below was seen by one investigator, and another investigator reported seeing a shadow in human form moving backwards and forwards behind one of the team members. As this session ended, the investigator which led the team downstairs thought she saw a figure hovering by the reception desk and described the figure as only being 3ft in height.

Toilet Corridor

It was in this area that reports had been made by staff of a woman being seen and a strong sense of unease being felt. One investigator felt their right buttock being touched while one of his colleagues was calling out for contact to be made. Another investigator reported seeing a short

Former staff reported a sense of unease on this staircase.

figure moving around the reception area, which mirrored the report made at the end of the session in the sky room and top gallery. One investigator felt that they caught a glimpse of a fleeting figure as they glanced up the stairs, and another reported seeing the light from outside increase in brightness. There were many fluctuations in electromagnetic field meter readings but the extractor fan in the men's toilet was found to cause these.

First-Floor Landing
One of the staff members that reported the case to the team said that she would always rush along this corridor as it made her feel very uncomfortable. During this session one investigator felt that someone had fallen down the stairs and another investigator reported a strong sense of general unease in this area. A rumbling sound was heard during this session that one team member interpreted as being male voices, but further exploration found that it was caused by traffic outside. At the end of the session, an investigator went to the use the bathroom on the ground floor and felt the overwhelming presence of a man.

Reception Area
It was decided that the final séance would be held in this area, due to two eyewitness accounts over the course of the evening suggesting that a short figure had been seen in this area. While asking for contact to be made, three clicks were heard by all investigators present.

Ending the Investigation
At the end of the investigation, the team had a debrief that also included the discussion of personal feelings which helped to ensure the members felt happy to leave and head for home. Each member was instructed to send back any video footage and images captured within the week for further analysis, as there is usually always a lot of information to gather from all the members before any final investigation report can be completed.

Results and Analysis
Non-vocal sounds were heard consistently by multiple investigators throughout the investigation. In fact, over one quarter of all reports were verified non-vocal noises; this is higher than the average total of all verified reports in an investigation. Various potentially natural explanations have been advanced for these cases, including the occasionally activated fan by the toilet doors, fireworks, or aircraft and traffic noises from outside.

There were several photographs that appeared to contain anomalies but, at second-stage analysis, these were ruled out as being natural in origin and caused by reflection, dust or equipment interference. There was one photo which, after going through first and second-stage analysis, still baffled analysts and was sent for third-stage analysis by one of the team's consultants. Interrogation of the EXIF data of the photograph showed an unusually long exposure time of four seconds. This long exposure allowed light to trail over the course of the seconds as the camera inevitably, as it was not on a tripod, moved. The light in this case derived from a video camera, represented as red-white light at the centre of the scene. The green-tint light derived from the colour of the walls. In this photograph the exposure was long and the light sources trailed because the flash unaccountably did not activate, not an uncommon problem with cameras. Shadows appeared to have been created because one of the two investigators in the shot moved, over the course of the

An eyewitness reported a sense of 'presence' in the toilet corridor.

four-second exposure, as verified by photographs immediately before and after this one was taken; precise times were extracted from the photographs' respective EXIF data so that this type of problem can be resolved.

There were three video clips that progressed to the second stage of analysis. In the first one, there were three distinct thuds caught on camera. The sounds were similar to that of pressure being placed on a wooden floor or step. It is possible that the floor or stairs were resettling following the movement of people involved in setting up the lock-off. In the second clip there were two moving orb-like objects seen on screen. Close examination of the footage revealed that the objects were insects illuminated by infra-red light from the camera. In the third piece of footage, there were several clicks heard on the video camera when it was in a lock-off session, but this was possibly a result of the auto-gain circuit, which can exaggerate camcorder sounds from far away if it is in a silent environment. This could also have been caused by the internal moving parts of the camera itself.

The report of battery drainage in the sky room and top gallery area is not an uncommon report made during investigations but, as this did not correlate with an increase in perceived paranormal activity, we must consider this to be a result of camera or battery malfunction. The flash of white light that was seen in this area may have been caused by the security light being activated outside, the flicker of the movement sensors on the floor below or fireworks which were seen and heard throughout the course of the night. The moving shadow seen behind an investigator was not repeatable but, as this was only witnessed by one investigator and was not objectively captured by camcorder, it is difficult to analyse this further.

When one investigator reported having his right buttock touched during a calling-out experiment, muscular movement may have caused this as he was standing up at the time. It is important that we do not read anything into the incident correlating with a calling-out experiment as it was only one positive 'hit' and was most likely to be coincidental in nature. The glimpse of a fleeting figure on the stairway was, again, only seen by one investigator and not captured by camera and may have been a result of changes in light caused by fireworks or the activation of the exterior security light. The perception reported by one investigator, of someone having fallen down the stairs, is of interest but has not been corroborated through historical accounts and may have been the result of expectation or context.

As with the buttock incident, there were not enough calling-out trials conducted in the reception area to know whether the clicks that were heard, when activity was asked for, were the result of anything more than chance. As already discussed this was an unusually, but naturally, noisy investigation and clicks were reported by investigators throughout the course of the night.

The short figure that was reported by two investigators on separate occasions is of interest, due to the fact that two people reported seeing the same thing. However, the investigators who reported these sightings were the interviewers who had conducted the staff witness interviews and were, therefore, aware that the building was once a children's home and that reports had been made of children being seen there. The effect of primed expectation must be considered as a likely contender, but this report does still seem to be of interest.

The perceptions reported during the Ganzfeld experiment do not obviously tally with the history of the site or previous reports that have been made, with the exception of the woman reported by one participant. The woman appeared to this participant twice – once on her own and once with a man behind her. The experiment was conducted in the area where the spectral woman had been reported by staff, but the description from the participant was too vague to enable us to suggest whether or not he was describing the figure that has been seen there. It is important to note that, at the time of taking part in the experiment, the investigator did not know that a woman was rumoured to haunt the building or that area specifically.

Conclusion

Olive House is a beautiful building that has been important to Swindon's community. Despite noise levels being quite high, in terms of perceptions this was a relatively quiet investigation, with a distinct lack of relevant footage being captured to shed further light on the reports made by staff who have worked there. The building has recently left the hands of Swindon Borough Council and developers have taken over its control. The future use of Olive House was unknown at the time of publication.

Investigation of Sally's Café, Highworth

Little did PSI realise the value of selecting a bin salesman as a new team member when running their 2006 recruitment drive. However, it has been through this new investigator that several cases for the *Haunted Swindon* project have been unearthed. Many investigation groups struggle to find venues to investigate but much homage must be paid to the suggestion that 'everyone has a ghost story to tell'. It may not have happened to them, it may have been a friend of a friend, but there are few people who you will encounter across the country who do not have some kind of tale to tell.

The problem is, of course, getting the stories told. Pop into any country pub, sit at the bar with the locals, bring up the subject of the paranormal and one can guarantee that yarn after yarn will be relayed until the landlord calls last orders. However, listening to people's encounters with the paranormal is something that PSI's newly-recruited investigator clearly had down to a fine art. It was while visiting Sally's Café on business in June 2007 that our investigator first heard of the owner's concerns regarding activity in her premises. Not wishing to prime himself by hearing the details, the investigator referred the case on to the PSI founders.

Interviewing the staff

In July 2007 a group founder met with the staff of Sally's Café to begin collating their accounts of unusual happenings within the building. Reports included electrical and mechanical interference, such as the temperature controller going up and down on the cooker, the dishwasher being mysteriously turned on and the oven timer going off without reason. Additionally, movement had been seen from the corner of the eye, a staff member reported being shoved as she climbed the stairs and a glass-fronted certificate was seen falling from the wall and smashing on the floor. Frequently the swing-door into the kitchen was heard to swing open and then slam shut. A loud thud was heard coming from the upstairs seating area and, upon inspection, a large suitcase had seemingly been flung across the room, knocking over a sugar bowl in its wake. It was in this same area that a staff member, on coming out of the bathroom, saw a tall, thin elderly gentleman stood in the middle of the room gazing at himself in the mirror, before simply vanishing.

Little is known about the history of the site, but prior to it becoming a coffee shop it had been a picture framing shop and it was rumoured that the then owner was fearful of the basement and rarely ventured down there. It is believed that the building is approximately 270 years old and is situated on the historic High Street of Highworth.

PSI Investigates

It was important that the team's investigation was conducted during normal working hours. As there were no accounts to support the assertion that activity might occur at the site when the shop is shut, the team needed to undertake their research during the time-frames at which activity had previously been reported.

In order to conduct a thorough site audit, it was necessary for the shop to be shut at the time of the investigation so that all areas could be thoroughly monitored and controlled. So as not to adversely effect the café's trade, the investigation was held on a Sunday afternoon when the shop was ordinarily shut. This did not allow entire ecological validity, as ideally the investigation would have occurred on both a day and at a time which the shop was usually open, but all other circumstances were matched as fully as possible.

Sallys, a delightful café on Highworth's historic High Street.

Due to the relatively small size of the venue, it was decided that the team would remain as one group. If the team had been in two groups, each group would have been within hearing range of one another and any incidences that occurred may have been misattributed as being caused by the other team. As few investigators were available to attend the investigation, due to summer holidays, this was an effective way of monitoring the site.

As previous experiences reported had been visual, kinetic and auditory in nature, the equipment used reflected these experiences. Video cameras, stills cameras and audio recording devices were deployed.

Investigators' Experiences

Within moments of arriving at the café, usual activity occurred. As the investigation leader and café owner went upstairs to unlock the office, the remainder of the team on the ground floor were treated to Geri Halliwell's rendition of *It's Raining Men* emanating from the CD player beneath the counter. Was it possible that the alleged ghost had a sense of humour? All of the remaining team, bar one, were male.

Over the course of the afternoon's investigation there were countless reports of investigators hearing what sounded like footsteps, clicks and taps. Three distinct thuds were also heard, but the team could not agree from which direction they originated. Faint music and muffled voices were also heard and bright flashes of light were seen by investigators when in the basement. As reported previously by venue staff, the group did discover the kitchen swing-door to be shut after they had left it open.

Examining the experiences

While the team has full access to the site they endeavour to unravel investigators' experiences as they occur. A coffee machine that was left on was found to be the culprit for the many clicks and taps that had been heard by the group. On exploring the perimeter of the building, neighbours in the garden of the adjacent property were identified as being the source of the murmured voices and a radio playing in the garden was the likely origin of the music that had been reported.

The flashes of light seen in the basement took a little longer to solve but, through redeploying two investigators to the ground floor and the rest of the group remaining in the basement, progress was made. It was theorised by the team that reflection from cars going past the shop windows could result in flashes of light crossing the shop floor and slipping beneath the door to the basement. With both groups of investigators linked via radios, the team in the basement radioed through to the investigators on the ground floor each time a flash of light was seen. The investigators on the ground floor were able to confirm that each time a flash was reported a car had gone past and a flash of light reflecting through the window had created the anomaly.

The group were greatly interested in discovering the kitchen swing-door to be shut, as this was something that staff had also experienced. In the case of the incident during the investigation, however, it was noted that the door was found to be shut after the basement door had been closed by the team. This could suggest, therefore, that the door swung shut as a result of the change in air current. To test this assumption the team congregated on the ground floor and filmed an investigator shutting the basement door and going up the stairs. This test was done repeatedly and, on each occasion, the swing-door did swing shut moments after the basement door was shut, which supports the theory that a change in air current might be responsible. What it does not resolve, however, are the staff member's accounts of the door slamming shut, as no noise was

The offending, allegedly self-activating, CD player.

made by the door during the team's trials. One factor that must be considered is the temperature on the day of the investigation. The investigation occurred in early August and the temperature was in the high 20s within the shop. This may have led to the door, being made of wood, swelling in the heat and the swelling of the wood may have softened the door's impact when it closed, resulting in no notable sound being made.

The high temperature is also thought to be to blame for the apparent sounds of footsteps heard on the floorboards. Most reports were made immediately after the floor had been crossed by the team and this is thought to be due to the wood expanding and settling in the heat.

The team were unable to explain, however, the mysterious playing of *It's Raining Men* on the CD player. The group were unable to identify any way to pre-set the player and there was no remote device that could have controlled it. The track that played was track three, and it is interesting to note that if it had turned on from standby it would not have defaulted to that track. The team tried pausing track three to see if would start playing automatically after a set period of time, but this did not occur. The investigation leader verified with the player's manufacturer that there was no means of programming or remotely controlling the device, so the cause of this phenomena remains unknown. A malfunctioning of the player cannot be ruled out as a possible cause.

There were no units of video or digital camera footage that contained anything for which the group could not account. On analysis, the investigation leaders were struck by how many sounds the team detected over the course of the investigation. These were resolved as being caused by the coffee machine and the effect of the high temperature on the building, but provided support for the new house effect theory. As previously mentioned, this theory purports that when someone enters a novel environment they attend to noises which normally go unnoticed by people who know the environment well. As people become accustomed to their surroundings they notice fewer and fewer natural sounds. If you live beside a busy road, chances are you tune out the drone of traffic and only notice it if someone else points it out.

To test this theory and to continue to try to understand what might be occurring at Sally's Café, the team paid a return trip.

Revisiting the scene

During the subsequent investigation, investigators continued to report experiences. An early thudding and rumbling sound was found to be caused by a car radio with a strong bass beat. A rapping heard on the window was blamed on a group of children that had congregated outside the building. A loud thud, perceived to be a heavy footfall, was explained by a car engine firing shortly afterwards, which suggested the thud may have been the closure of the car door.

There were several reports made by individual investigators which may be physiological in nature. One investigator reported a tingling sensation, while another felt a drop in temperature. These two incidents were only reported by individual investigators and, with it being unique to them, they may have been caused by physiological factors. There was a report made by one investigator of seeing a small black shape glide across her field of vision. This was possibly caused by a dead cell in her eye crossing her vision, known as a floater.

The sound of cutlery clattering together was reported by one investigator but was not objectively recorded by audio recorder or camera and was not confirmed by other investigators. A 'boing' sound was heard by two investigators in the basement and the freezer was isolated as the cause of this.

Several thumps were heard on the floorboards on the ground floor while investigators were in the basement. This coincided with investigators calling out for contact. It would be irresponsible to suggest that this was a result of anything other than chance, as not enough trials were conducted to prove significance. The fact that the floorboards had recently been walked upon was identified as the most likely cause of the phenomena, due to the time needed for wood to resettle.

Many investigators said that they felt the atmosphere was oppressive. The impact of suggestion, the forming of group norms and effect of social desirability must all be considered as influencing factors. One investigator felt that they picked up on an angry energy in the building and a connection with Victorian sail boats and the Navy. The group have not been able to corroborate this report with any historical evidence and it must remain as an unconfirmed subjective experience.

On the return visit the group did not report hearing the clicks and taps that had been detected on the first visit. However, when consciously listening for these sounds, they were still present. This supports the new house effect as the group had, by now, become more familiar with their environment.

In regard to experiences that had been reported by staff, no kinetic activity was observed during the two investigations. The glass-framed certificate falling from the wall could possibly have been caused by traffic vibrations from the high street, but no cause has been identified for the report of the suitcase seemingly having been flung across the first floor.

The boxes on the first floor.

With the exception of the CD player incident, no mechanical malfunctions were reported by the team during the two investigations and further enquiry by the machines' manufacturers may be required to shed more light on these occurrences.

The identity of the man seen on the first floor remains a mystery and, as no investigator experienced the shoving sensation reported by a member of staff, no firm conclusions can be drawn. The effect of a muscle spasm must, however, be considered.

Corner-of-eye movement has been reported by both staff members and by investigators. With the majority of these occurrences being in the left field of vision, it is possible these were caused by neurological factors; research into this is currently being conducted by leading academics.

Conclusions
Ongoing contact with Sally's Café reveals that activity is continuing. While the team were successful in identifying many natural causes of the phenomena reported, questions do remain unanswered. The team looks forward to maintaining their relationship with the venue and hopes to shed further light on the case in the future.

INVESTIGATION OF THE JOLLY TAR AT HANNINGTON

Research into the Jolly Tar started as a result of idle conversation, as is so often the case when discovering new accounts of phenomena. One of PSI's investigators casually dropped into his conversation with the pub's landlord that, in his spare time, he was a paranormal investigator. This sparked great curiosity in the landlord, who then went on to explain that, since taking over the premises, he and his family had been having encounters they simply could not understand.

Not wishing to prime himself in advance of any investigation, the PSI investigator explained to the landlord that he would ask the group's founders to visit the pub to conduct witness interviews that might lead onto further investigation and research. On receiving this report in late 2006, the founders then followed up on what was going to be the first of many of the *Haunted Swindon* project's cases.

Background and Witness Interviews

The interviews, conducted on 14 December 2006, revealed that there was indeed a diverse mix of phenomena being experienced. Six days prior to the interviews taking place, the landlord reported that, while stoking the fire in the lounge bar, he happened to look up and saw what he described as being a middle-aged man of about 5ft 10in and wearing old clothes. The experience lasted mere seconds.

Could this be the same man that his wife had seen just days before? The landlady recounted how she had been sitting in the public bar with her husband (the landlord) and her son (the chef) when she suddenly became aware of a man standing to the right of the fireplace, alongside the dartboard. Again, he was around 5ft 10in and was seen to be wearing a long dark coat. His face,

The Jolly Tar became a public house in 1855.

head and hair appeared to be blurred, but grey in colour. Following on from this sighting, the landlady noticed that on the days subsequent to his appearance the picture above the fireplace would often be found to be skewed. Her son, the chef, went on to recall how he too had seen a man matching that description the day before his mother had. While sitting in the public bar, he was aware of somebody who had come into the pub and made their way towards the bar. He said that the figure was, again, around 5ft 10in and wore dark clothing. When he turned to see where the person had gone, there was nobody there.

Whoever the man making appearances is, he has not limited his exposure to just the pub staff. Over the years there have been several accounts of a man matching his description being seen in the dartboard area of the public bar. It has also been suggested that this man has a female companion. According to the accounts of two startled customers, they were enjoying a meal by the fireplace in the lounge bar when, to their shock and horror, an old lady appeared to walk out of the fireplace. Distressed by their encounter, they promptly got up and left without paying, only to return a few days later to explain what had happened.

It is not only apparitions that the Jolly Tar can treat us to. One evening, while in the private upstairs lounge, the landlord and chef watched in amazement as a bag from a box of wine was seemingly swept off of the table and onto the floor. With no evidence of drafts, or other possible explanations, the pair were left perplexed.

After the official PSI interviews were conducted, phenomena continued with gusto. On going into his bedroom upstairs, the chef was shocked to discover a series of £1 coins stood neatly on edge on a rickety wicker surface. He has tried repeatedly to re-enact the arrangement but has been unsuccessful. Further evidence to suggest that the phenomena may have taken a kinetic turn includes early morning cleaning staff encountering beer mats strewn across the lounge bar floor, when they had been safely on tables at closing time.

History of the Jolly Tar

In order to gain an insight into the history of the Jolly Tar, PSI enlisted the assistance of its resident historical researcher to try and shed some light on the past.

The pub, situated in the small village of Hannington on the outskirts of Swindon, is a Grade II listed building that started its life as an 18th-century farmhouse. It became a public house in 1855 and its name, meaning jolly sailor, was chosen in recognition of the marriage of Captain Willes Johnson and the widow of Colonel Freke. The Freke family were well-known and highly regarded within the village, and their memory lives in the pub named after them at the mouth of the village.

There is little by way of ill-fate reported in the history of the Jolly Tar. Hearsay, however, suggests that the carpenter who hung the sign for the pub committed suicide after returning home from the pub to discover his wife having an affair with a local farmer.

Between 1855 and 1922, the pub played host to a variety of inn-keeping families before being purchased by a local brewery, Arkells.

PSI Investigates

After having completed the witness interviews, the PSI founders deduced that the majority of reported activity occurred during daylight hours. Due to investigators' availability and brewery restrictions, it was going to be difficult to investigate the Jolly Tar solely at the times that activity was reported, thus adhering to ecological validity at its utmost. Through negotiation, the team were

The Jolly Tar is an example of virtually undocumented oral tradition being passed down word-for-word for over a century.

able to secure a time at which both the pub was shut and phenomena had been previously encountered.

On the afternoon of 21 January 2007 the PSI team arrived at the Jolly Tar to be greeted by the landlord and landlady. As the rest of the team started to assemble equipment and resources, the founders explained the format the investigation was going to take and answered any remaining questions that the proprietors had.

With the staff members fully briefed, they retired to the private living quarters to allow the

team to commence its work. The investigation began with a walk through the building so that investigators could familiarise themselves with the layout and be notified of any health and safety concerns. As usual, an extraneous factors audit was completed to help the team eliminate potential natural causes of phenomena or irregularities that might later appear on film or in evidence. The team was also told what the pub staff had previously reported.

It is often thought that it is preferable for investigators to go into an investigation *tabula rasa* in regard to others' prior experiences, for it is feared that any priming may result in skewed investigator reports. This priming may lead investigators to see more in a situation than is actually there, or may warp their perceptions to support previously made claims. In this case, however, PSI decided that, in order to most effectively investigate the phenomena being reported, the team had to know what they were looking for. For example – was the man who was being seen by the dartboard actually just being created by a mixture of shadows and car headlights descending the nearby hill? If the team did not know that a man was meant to be seen there, then they would not have known to look out for this phenomenon and its potential causes.

Through witness interviews the team had identified two key areas of activity: the public bar and the lounge bar. With this in mind, the team split into two groups to monitor these areas. Due to the nature of the reported phenomena being primarily visual, the equipment used reflected the need of the investigation. Video cameras and stills cameras were provided to both teams as ways of potentially capturing the reported activity.

While PSI has an arsenal of environmental and auditory monitoring equipment at its disposal, the use of such equipment could not be justified as no phenomena within the equipment's scope of measurement had been reported. If sudden drops in temperature or the sound of voices had been reported then environment meters and audio recorders would have been enlisted.

With the teams split in half, each group retreated to their first area. In the lounge bar, the group set up beer mats on tables and focused a video camera on them throughout the session to try and capture any movement. A second video camera was set up to film the the whole room including the team. Meanwhile, the second group set up a video camera to focus on the dartboard area of the public bar and another camera, again, to capture their scene.

During the sessions the teams were required to note down any experiences that the team or individual members of the team had, as well as being responsible for the taking of photographs to try and catch the apparitions (or the causes of perceived apparitions) which were reputed to haunt the areas under surveillance.

Both teams spent 45 minutes in their respective areas before stopping for a refreshment break. The investigation then recommenced, with the teams swapping the areas that they had been monitoring. This format was followed for several hours, ensuring that both teams had sufficiently covered both areas. At one point, one team halved again when loud banging could be heard coming from the store-room adjacent to the public bar. Two members of that team went into the store-room to try and identify the source of the banging, but it discontinued upon their entry and they were unable to discover its cause.

After both the public and private bars had been covered exhaustively by the teams, it was time for the pub to open for its evening customers. The team acknowledged that previous encounters with phenomena had occurred while staff members were going about their daily business, rather than when they were specifically trying to capture activity. It was decided, therefore, that the team should engage in naturalistic observation of the pub. This meant that investigators had to remove all evidence of the investigation and anything that identified them as being investigators.

Again, split into two groups, the team bought themselves soft drinks and blended into the pub environment to watch the pub in its natural state, with locals propping up the bar and staff busy at work. Cameras were concealed in team members' clothing, ready to be brought out in case of any paranormal appearances. After monitoring the pub in its natural condition, the team slipped out unnoticed, ready to undertake hours of footage analysis in the hope of coming one step closer towards understanding the activity at the Jolly Tar. It was unfortunate that nothing was observed that prompted the use of the video camera while observing naturalistically. However, it was also fortunate as, ethically, it is reasonable to observe a pub full of people but bringing out a video camera is ethically insensitive.

Investigators' Experiences

During the course of the first investigative visit, team members reported a variety of personal experiences. On entering the public bar from behind the bar, two team members reported sensations on their heads and faces – a sense of pressure and tingling. These team members also reported a great sense of expectation in the air. Corner-of-eye movement behind the bar was also reported as the particular team member felt that something was touching her hair.

Two investigators reported that they could see nondescript low-level movement in both bars, synonymous with what might be seen if a spectral cat or dog was present. These investigators were in separate groups and did not share their experiences until after the investigation.

One team heard a series of bangs and knocks seemingly originating from the store-room and, while the knocks stopped on investigation, one of the investigators entering the store-room felt a stroking sensation on his head, followed by pins and needles for approximately 30 seconds. Both team members investigating the store-room felt a presence behind them and both turned to look at the door at the same time, as though someone was standing there.

Other reports included a moustachioed gentleman being seen looking into the pub from the outside although, on inspection, no one was present, a small blue light appearing on a brass pot in the lounge bar, blue lights being seen sporadically in the public bar and a shadow being seen to move across the restaurant area. Further accounts from the team included the movement of whiteness behind the bar, along with a shadowy figure and a fleeting figure being seen behind the bar by a couple of investigators.

Due to the quantity and quality of reports being made, the team felt that a return trip to the pub would be justified and this was set up for a week later.

PSI's return trip

To replicate the environment in which the team had had their initial encounters, the team revisited the Jolly Tar one week later, at exactly the same time and for the same duration, in an attempt to understand and explain both their own experiences from the week before and the enduring encounters of the staff.

On the return trip, the same format was followed as on the initial visit. In addition, however, video cameras were also used to monitor behind the empty bar, in recognition of the accounts made where figures and movement were seemingly seen in this area.

During this second visit, the team was once again treated to what appeared to be a variety of potentially unusual phenomena. In the public bar, the sense of anticipation was once again apparent. In addition, scraping noises were heard that were compared to the sound of a beer mat being scraped across the bar, and a spotlight above the bar dimmed momentarily. A chair was heard to creak, as though someone had sat down on it, and one investigator reported a crushing sensation against their head. Someone was seen to poke their head around the corner from the conservatory into the lounge bar, but nobody could be found, and another figure was perceived to walk behind the bar and dip into the small store-room situated halfway between the two bars. A swirling white light was also seen to appear above another investigator's head while in the vicinity of the dartboard area. It was reported that at around 5pm there was a noticeable change in atmosphere in the pub when it suddenly felt 'heavier'; this was acknowledged by most of the team. During this period of oppression, figure-like movement was seen in the peripheral vision of many of the team, but nothing focused.

Psychic Impression

Psychic or sensitive impressions are reported by PSI in appreciation of the team's diversity in belief and recognition of the potential phenomena. During the Jolly Tar investigations, several pieces of information were provided by team members, including the names Jonathan and Abraham, as having a connection with the building and the perception of a man named William Dreyfuss, who is seen pacing behind the bar and is connected to someone called Mollie Tanner. Additionally, one investigator had dreamt about the pub before investigating it and, despite having never visited the pub previously, she claimed that the pub was exactly the same as it was in her dream. In her dream she had also seen a scruffy, dark-haired man pacing behind the bar.

Analysing the evidence

There was little by way of photographic evidence to excite the analysts after PSI's two visits to the Jolly Tar. A photograph portraying a misty mass provided temporary enthusiasm until it was suggested that residual cigarette smoke, prior to the ban, could not be ruled out as being the culprit.

Light anomalies on stills pictures were analysed and understood to be caused by reflective surfaces and the effect of pinpricks of light (e.g. LED bulbs) being dragged across shots by the camera flash.

Units of video footage, however, were of greater interest. The sound of smashing glass was heard on one of the cameras but its visual recording did not capture any breaking glass and no evidence of this having happened was heard or discovered by the investigation team at the time. While the exact cause of the sound has not been established, it must be borne in mind that staff members were present in the above living quarters. Another segment of video footage included intermittent popping sounds. Again, no direct cause has been identified, but the internal workings of the camera and the possibility of heaters or other electrical equipment must be considered as potential sources. A further unit of video footage showed the camera having difficulty in finding focus. This is most often caused by something moving into the camera's field of vision and confusing its ability to focus. This can, however, be caused by small, insignificant air-borne particles.

Conclusion

During PSI's two trips to the Jolly Tar, video and photographic footage failed to provide any significant evidence in support of the reported phenomena. What remains interesting, however, is the vast array of subjective experiences reported by team members. The banging in the store-room was of great interest, especially as numerous team members heard it, although it was not captured on camera. What needs to be realised, however, is that the team only amassed nine hours of site time over the two investigations and this is not deemed to be a sufficient amount of time to truly understand the pub, its natural noises and any shifts or changes that may naturally occur in an old building.

The team member's dream, seemingly about the pub and the man that has been seen, in advance of the investigation, remains of interest, but no conclusions can be drawn from it due to the uncontrolled environment in which the information was relayed. Similarly the sensitive, or psychic, information that team members relayed during the investigation was, again, provided in an uncontrolled environment and cannot be considered within the team's scientific methodology.

The information remains of interest but no conclusive link can be drawn between the information and the Jolly Tar.

There were several reports by team members suggesting that they were aware of fleeting figures and movement, primarily seen from the corner of their eye. While no physical cause for this phenomenon could be identified, hallucination cannot be ruled out, nor can the wider evidence to suggest that the human mind can have a tendency to erroneously sense movement in its peripheral vision. The failure to capture this reported activity on video means that there is no objective evidence to support team members' claims.

It is also important to reiterate that, due to the nature of the phenomena being experienced by staff, PSI did tell its team members what had been previously experienced. While PSI feels that this decision was justified in this case, we must recognise the potential effect of primed expectation on investigators and the heightened sense of anticipation that may have led team members to note occurrences which might otherwise have passed without comment.

Ongoing contact with the pub staff has suggested that the phenomena are still continuing daily, up until the point that the landlord and landlady leave the pub, but due to the lack of opportunity for a sustained period of investigation, it is difficult for PSI to draw any conclusions as to whether or not the Jolly Tar is haunted.

INVESTIGATION OF THE PINEHURST COMMUNITY CENTRE

As a former employee of the Swindon Children's Scrapstore, I was aware that the site of the Pinehurst People's Centre, containing Scrapstore and the Pinehurst Community Centre, was no stranger to reports of anomalous experiences. Indeed, during my own time at the Scrapstore I had several personal encounters at the site.

While sat at my desk, I observed the stooped form of a woman shuffle past the door leading out to the corridor but, upon inspection, there was nobody there. I would come into work in the morning to find items from the art and craft shop strewn across the middle of the floor. With no roads surrounding the building it is unlikely it was caused by traffic vibrations and no other causes were ever identified. The most chilling of all, however, was the overwhelming sense of presence in the main Scrapstore hall when locking up at night. On many nights I hot-footed it across the hall after switching out the lights, acutely aware of the sensation of being watched and feeling the air thicken. It was these personal experiences that inspired me to ask other personnel at the site whether they had had any experiences.

A Scrapstore volunteer reported that she had heard that a woman allegedly haunted the whole site, and the building's security staff confirmed that there had been reports of a spectral woman being seen in the corridors. It was not until I ventured down to the adjoining Pinehurst Community Centre, however, that I discovered that there was a lot more to this case than I could ever have imagined.

Eyewitness Interviews

In March 2007 I was fortunate to meet with volunteers from the Pinehurst Community Centre (PCC) who were all very willing to share their site experiences with me. Human figures had been seen in the top corridor leading towards the office. A mist and a male figure were both seen by the toilets, but did not appear on the CCTV footage for that area. One volunteer claimed to have been mysteriously scratched on her hand, while another lady came into the office and spoke at great length with a gentleman well-known in the area – only to discover later that he had died some five years earlier. Three black figures had been seen standing in the Olive Branch bar attached to the PCC and lights in the main hall had been turned on and off, seemingly of their own accord. These incidents were of great interest to

The Olive Branch bar.

the *Haunted Swindon* project team but time was not our side, as the site was set to be demolished to make way for a new academy.

History of the Centre

Through gaining an understanding of the site's history, the team hoped to identify any factors that could contribute towards people's experiences. This could include unearthing disturbing information about the site, such as any unnatural deaths that might have occurred there, which might shape witnesses' perceptions and possibly lead to misinterpretation of events as a result of primed expectation. Similarly it could allow us to detect structural factors which might influence or contribute towards experiences.

The building which is now that of the PCC was previously occupied by the Pinehurst Secondary School between 1936 and 1986. Prior to this, information from an Ordnance Survey map of 1887 suggests that the land was open countryside adjacent to Hurst Farm, within the parish of Rodbourne Cheney. At the time of the Domesday Book, the landowner has been identified as being Reginald and the earlier Saxon landowner was Miles Crispin. In 1928 the parish of Rodbourne Cheney was incorporated into the Borough of Swindon.

Upon the closure of the school in 1986, the site was split into the Pinehurst Community Centre and the Pinehurst People's Centre and has been at the heart of the Pinehurst community ever since.

PSI Investigates

Due to the short notice at which this investigation was called, the imminent closure of the site and the small number of hours that the team could arrange for access, this investigation was classified as fieldwork. The study would focus on investigators attempting to identify the causes of the reported activity through exposure to the site.

The team paid two visits to the site, once in March 2007 and a follow-up in May 2007. Team members were not told what experiences had been previously reported in advance of the investigation as the leaders did not want to prime them with what to expect. However, both investigation leaders were aware of previous reports at the site and this allowed them to effectively direct and deploy personnel and resources to key areas.

One investigation leader was responsible for leading the team of investigators through their study of the site, while the other leader was stationed in the office and studied live CCTV footage as the investigation unravelled. Both leaders were connected via radios and this allowed them to relay information to one another and to seek clarification of events as they were viewed remotely. This methodology, towards which the team are striving, resources allowing, enables the site to be monitored at all times and allows the viewer the opportunity to identify factors which may be contributing towards investigators' experiences during the investigation. Similarly, investigators can call upon the viewer to focus the cameras on a certain area if they believe activity may be occurring and a natural resolution may be identified.

It was important that the investigations were conducted at times when the centre was usually open as it was during these hours that experiences had been reported. As such, the research was conducted between the hours of 5pm and 11pm, during which time the centre closed for the team, but it is important to note that the neighbouring Olive Branch bar was open and that the public had access to the exterior of the site throughout the two nights of investigation.

Over the course of the first investigation, as mentioned earlier, one investigation leader remained in the office to view live CCTV footage with two other investigators, while the other leader and the remainder of the team spent 45-minute sessions in the corridor, the main hall and the Vickery suite. These were all areas in which activity had been reported by centre staff as, due to the relatively small amount of time that the team had access to the site, they could not justify investigating areas in which no reports had been made. Had more time been available to the team, it would have been advisable to have studied a control location – a room which had had no previous reports of activity – to allow the team to understand whether the previous reports were location or person-specific in nature.

Over the course of the two investigations, the team used video and digital stills cameras to attempt to capture any occurrences which were perceived as paranormal in nature. It was decided not to use environmental monitoring equipment as none of the reported experiences had an obvious potential environmental origin or cause.

Investigators' Experiences

The first night of investigation was 16 March 2007. Over the course of this investigation there were several reports made by team members in the investigation group. These included the sense of unease in the Vickery suite, accompanied by a moving light across the wall. One investigator claims to have seen a figure walk through the door into a locked cupboard by the male toilets. Three investigators felt uncomfortable when looking into the children's playroom beyond the Vickery suite. All of the investigation team heard the shuddering/juddering of the grate in the kitchen serving-hatch located off the corridor. The CCTV viewers reported the movement of light and human shadows in the corridor, as well as CCTV equipment malfunction, and intermittency of the tick of the clock in the office.

The Pinehurst Community Centre is being demolished to make way for an academy.

What appeared to be of greatest interest during this first investigation was the movement of a coat on a dress rail in the Vickery suite. While the team were sitting observing the room, they became aware that the hanger on which the coat was hanging was slowly rotating. The investigation team vacated the area and left a video camera recording the scene. Ten minutes after the team had left, the camera caught the coat rotating 90 degrees on the rail once more. Further study into this phenomenon was conducted at the subsequent investigation.

The Team Returns

Due to a number of unexplainable incidents occurring during the first night of research, the team paid a return visit on 4 May 2007 to try and resolve the unanswered questions.

The investigation followed the same format as the first visit, with one team leader co-ordinating the investigation team while the other leader observed the site and investigation remotely through the use of CCTV.

During this return trip, investigators continued to report experiences which included the movement of a dark shape in the Vickery suite, the sound of a giggling child coming from the playroom and ongoing reports of the kitchen grate rattling. Investigators continued to report a sense of ill-ease in the area of the children's playroom and the feeling of a heavy atmosphere. The CCTV viewer reported hearing an intermittent dull thudding sound throughout the first hour of the night.

Much of this return visit focused on identifying the causes of the rattling grate and the rotating coat hanger, which we will consider further in our analysis.

Psychic Impressions

While mediumship is of interest to the group, PSI believes these need to be measured in a controlled environment rather than in an investigation setting. As PSI is interested in these impressions gleaned by investigators through unknown sources, perhaps psychically, we do note them in our investigation reports. However, we cannot vouch for their credibility or validity and no conclusions can be drawn from them.

During the first investigation, one investigator perceived a person scrambling or crawling along the corridor, appearing frightened, heading away from the children's playroom. Another investigator, also in the area of the playroom, sensed the presence of a teenage girl walking quickly away from somebody, seemingly terrified. An interpretation of these events is considered in our analysis.

Analysing the Evidence

The most compelling incidents of the two evenings of study were the moving coat and the rattling kitchen grate, as these incidents were captured objectively on film and witnessed by all present. During the group's return visit, they spent much time investigating these occurrences in greater depth.

In regard to the moving coat, it was initially thought this was caused by investigators walking past the coat and that the movement of air caused the rotation. However, this theory was quashed when the coat was captured on video camera moving of its own accord 10 minutes after investigators had left the room. When trying to replicate this incident, the team discovered that the change in air current in the adjoining corridor, caused by the closing of a corridor door, was

An entrance to the centre.

enough to recreate this event and the team were successful in doing so over numerous trials. The mystery of the rattling kitchen grate was also resolved this way. The team monitored the kitchen grate as investigators tried opening and closing various doors, in a systematic manner, along the length of the corridor and the grate did shudder and rattle as a result of the change of air current. This test was repeated several times with identical results.

There were many accounts of investigators feeling uncomfortable in the playroom area. Our understanding of the psychology of anomalous experience tells us that, as investigators were openly verbalising their discomfort, they could have been unintentionally implanting the sense of unease in other investigators and the power of suggestion cannot be ruled out. The effect of group conformity and social desirability must also be considered.

There were several reports of changing volumes of light but these were identified, through the use of CCTV, as being caused by several external sources including car headlights, a torch and security lighting. CCTV was also successful in identifying the source of the reported giggling child as being a group of teenage girls congregated outside the building.

When the CCTV operator reported seeing moving human shadows, the investigation team were able to ascertain that these were being caused by the reflection of people in the Olive Branch bar being cast through the adjoining window. Similarly, when the CCTV operator detected an intermittent thudding sound, the investigation team were able to deduce that it was being caused by boys kicking a football against one of the site's walls, which was not monitored by CCTV.

The malfunctioning of the CCTV system was confirmed by site staff as not being unusual and resulted from it being an old system. The report of the ticking of the clock being irregular was recognised as being caused by the effect of attention in novel environments. More often than not, the sound of the tick was tuned out as there were other stimuli to which the operator was attending, but when there was a deficit of other stimuli the operator became aware of the tick once more. This was tried and tested by different investigators sitting in the office and consciously attending to the ticking clock and confirming the regularity of its tick.

The reports of seeing a man walk into the locked cupboard, the perceived impressions of a frightened figure crawling along the corridor and a girl walking away terrified do remain of interest to the group but, as they are purely subjective in nature and are without any corroborating evidence, it is difficult to analyse these further. It is possible that the two investigators who reported these incidents may have primed one another through their reports as both impressions relate to somebody being frightened and trying to get away from the playroom area. Similarly, the investigators' own anxiety about the playroom area could have been a factor that influenced the psychic impressions that they reported. It is interesting to note, however, that the report of the man in the corridor area correlates with previous eyewitness reports from site volunteers of which the investigator was not aware, although no conclusions can be drawn without accompanying objective evidence.

Other human forms have also been identified by both investigators and site volunteers, but in the case of the investigators it was found to be caused by shadows of people outside of the building or through the window of the nearby bar. These causes should be considered as explanations for the original eyewitness accounts as well.

The team did not encounter any scratches appearing on investigators or the switching on and off of lights, which had all been reported by site volunteers. An accidental and unnoticed graze of the skin may account for the original report of receiving a scratch at the site and an electrical fault may have been responsible for the irregularities with the lighting. However, without being able to investigate these incidents as they occurred and without objective evidence, it is not possible to deduce definite causes.

Aside from the video footage of the coat moving, there were no other units of video footage which withstood first-stage analysis. There were clicks and taps heard on the tape, but these have been detected before and identified as being caused by the moving parts inside the video camera.

One stills photograph did contains white spherical shapes – known as orbs – but, as a result of the team's exhaustive research into the orb phenomena, PSI can conclude that such photos are caused by out-of-focus dust particles.

Conclusion

This investigation showed the team the value of being able to remotely view an investigation environment through the use of CCTV. It facilitated PSI in understanding and detecting misinterpreted events and allowed the whole site to be monitored when there were not enough personnel to physically cover the area. Generally, it allows an investigation environment to be monitored without human intervention, as the mere presence of investigators introduces alien factors which can be difficult to control.

The team were successful in identifying many causes of their own experiences at the site, but some reports by investigators and site volunteers remain unexplained. With the building now vacant and due for demolition, it is unlikely that we will ever get to the bottom of this fascinating case.

INVESTIGATION OF A PRIVATE WOOD, NORTH SWINDON

A privately-owned wood in north Swindon is a little-known location that has been the subject of many ghost stories in times gone by and continues to elicit some of Swindon's strangest stories to this day. The name of the wood has been withheld, as there is a recent history of trespassing, and it would be unethical to encourage more by naming the site.

History of the Site

The site is an isolated wood with no significant roads nearby, although access is provided by tracks and footpaths including some designated as a public right of way. It is a roughly rectangular strip of woodland that lies along the boundary of the modern town of Swindon (to the west) and Wiltshire, set in slightly undulating countryside in the Thames valley. Comparison of a modern Ordnance Survey map with one dated 1885 shows that the wood has grown, almost doubling its size. There is a spring or reservoir near the north-western tip of the wood and the 1885 map shows a building, perhaps a barn, approximately 260m south of that spring. A footpath appears to have led from this building to a farm, but both the building and the footpath have now disappeared. There have been a number of artefacts dating to the Bronze and Iron Ages found in the vicinity, with a notable clustering around 3km north near the Thames/Isis river at Castle Eaton. However, there are four prehistoric circular enclosures within 750m to the south and west of the site.

The Domesday survey (1086) shows that Odo (half brother of William I) held half the lordship of the local manor, and the other half of the manor was held by the Drews family. When Odo fell out of political favour, his holdings returned to the Crown, and the land was entrusted to the Prater family. The Prater dynasty is known to have continued its association with the area, with many members being born and buried there, at least until the mid-17th century.

In the early 20th century the district was a favourite one with fox hunters and there was a meet nearby where traditional fences and ditches were perilous enough to test the mettle of both horse and rider, and where wire fences were becoming a hazard.

A wood in north Swindon.

Legends of the Site

There are several distinct legends associated with the wood. The first tells of the site being haunted by the ghost of a murdered man. The man, himself a drover, was said to have been slain by another drover on the way back from the market; the dispute was said to have been over how much money had been made that day. Another story tells that the last keeper haunts the wood. He was said to have been killed when attacked by poachers in the wood. The keeper's cottage could be the building identified on the 1885 map, which has since been cleared away.

One local landowner recounted a story about the wood that had been passed through his family for generations. He reported that there was meant to be a headless horseman who gallopped through the woods. He also reported that when shooting in the wood his dogs would suddenly go berserk, behaving strangely and seemingly chasing nothing.

So far the story is not entirely unusual. Woods are often held to be spooky places, particularly in low lighting, and ghost stories often develop with a warning that supports societal norms. In this case children may well be told the story to keep them away from the dangerous woods at night.

Researchers from the Highworth Historical Society have also heard rumours that the site was once meant to be a moonrakers' site. The moonrakers' legend is a famous Wiltshire story. The story goes that local brandy smugglers would hide barrels of brandy in ponds to avoid being prosecuted. Later they would be caught raking the pond to find the barrels; however, upon being caught they would deviously claim to be raking for cheese (actually the reflection of the moon). In societal terms this story is meant to represent that, while Wiltshire residents are perceived as being dim-witted, they are in fact cleverer than they appear.

Recent Eyewitness Experiences

Accounts from people in 2006 and 2007 who had wondered off the public footpath into the private wood provide a story that definitely borders on the weird. One of them told the PSI:

'I have been in myself and so have other north Swindon residents. This place is one of the scariest I have encountered. You see things, hear things and, every time you go back to it, the forest changes inside. There once was a pond in it but after returning there was no traces of it. There have also been reports of big cages and tree houses inside. Giant paw prints have been found within the fields surrounding it and children's footsteps. The place is deserted so can't understand it. If you talk to the nearby residents, they say they would not even attempt to go there as they have seen a man on a horse galloping alongside the dirt track that leads up to it. I would certainly never go back.'

These accounts bring us into areas of paranormal studies. Finding 'giant paw prints' tends to point towards the study of alien big cats; alien in the sense of not being native to the country of sighting, rather than being extra-terrestrial in nature! Although documented sightings and evidence span the centuries, the subject of alien big cats has gained popularity and prominence in the UK since the 1960s. Somewhat unconvincing explanations have surfaced, including survivors from the prehistoric past, where big cats were native to the UK, a form of animal unknown to science, and creatures of supernatural origin. Other theories have suggested that there is a certain number of breeding big cats that either escaped or were released during the 1960s and 1970s when it was legal to keep such animals privately. Similarly, some researchers believe such big cats were released into the wild when the Dangerous Wild Animals Act (1976) made keeping such beasts illegal. On a more realistic level, misattribution of sightings and evidence is reported to be fairly commonplace. Such paw prints might have been exaggerated in the memory and might relate to any number of large animals native in the UK. Interestingly, while PSI was investigating this case the local newspaper, the *Swindon Advertiser*, reported on a 'big cat' story in the area. The 'big cat' – actually no larger than a household cat – turned out to be an imported, domestic cat.

The other accounts of finding animal cages in different levels of use and the interior appearing to alter on different visits is a less easy phenomenon to classify. The closest anomalous studies, material to these experiences, that the authors could find were of time slips. Time slips are said to be a type of anomalous phenomena in which the experiencers, through supernatural and unintentional means, travel through time. Time slips experiencers typically report walking through an (often familiar) location, feeling a certain sense of unreality and then walking 'through the past': literally seeing their environment not as it should be now, but as (they speculate) it would once have been in times gone past. The accounts of finding changed landscapes and finding bird cages, either disused and broken down or in full life and storing wildlife, rather awkwardly fit into this pattern, with reservations. Needless to say there is no scientific evidence of time slips or any such reality shifts, and more sceptical researchers would suggest hallucinations are to blame.

The experiencer also claimed to have found a pool of water on one occasion, but not on another occasion. It is worth pointing out that this wood and surrounding area is incredibly susceptible to flooding, and experience would suggest it would take only a modest storm to create an impressive pool that would take days to drain away. The final report was of a second-hand account of seeing a galloping horseman. As previously established, this is a fairly popular local legend.

Fieldwork Investigations

By their very nature, fieldwork trips are very different from formal investigations. Certain locations – particularly outdoors – are almost impossible to control. In a standard building you can place certain controls on the environment and monitor it in such a way as to be fully aware what the causes of any disturbances may be. In an outdoor location there are so many variables at play that it is impossible to attempt to control them to any degree of satisfaction. As such, fieldwork becomes a process of observation using photography and videography to provide objective back-up.

The scientific value of such methods is debatable. PSI believes that it is still possible to try to locate potential natural variables that could account for anomalous experiences. Furthermore, the research questions that arise from observing such natural environments are of great value to our research unit.

The First Investigation

The first of the PSI team's two fieldwork trips, in June 2007, saw six investigators spend several hours on site with the prior agreement with the landowner. Previous reports of strange incidences were reported as all having happened during the evening, so the team-planning session resolved to match these circumstances. During the first hours of the fieldwork daylight illuminated the wood, but soon after the sun set the thick wood was in complete darkness.

On entering the wood the group found a clearing approximately 50ft north north-east of the entrance to the wood, at which point three members of the group experienced feeling light-headed and uneasy. One investigator reported withdrawing himself from the group assuming he was unwell and the only person feeling the sensation. Each was surprised to discover that the other had felt the same sensation at the same time.

Keeping in touch with two-way radio units, the group split into two teams to traverse two sectors of the wood. Each team spent time observing each area that had been associated with past experiences. The first team located and documented the animal cage. The cage was broken down and disused; the area was overgrown and the mesh entangled. Meanwhile, the second team spent further time on the perimeter and surrounding tracks, where experiences had been reported. During this time four of the six investigators did not report any unusual events. One investigator reported the sound of what was perceived as bells ringing. On investigation of the nearby field, it was discovered that the movement of the corn in the wind could have produced a similar sound.

Another investigator described a brief unusual experience: 'I saw what looked like a face in the bushes. My position at the time was at the iron gates at the entrance to the wood. The face appeared to be 200 yards from my position at right angles to the gates. After 30 seconds the face disappeared. There were no discernable features just a flesh coloured oval shape.'

No level of analysis of video footage revealed anything out of the ordinary. One stills photograph outside of the wood showed a thick, billowing mist on what was a clear summer early evening. The photograph coincided with a break taken by team members where an investigator, standing with their back to the resting photographer, lit a cigarette. Previous experience has demonstrated that even a small amount of smoke close to the camera lens can be illuminated by the flash and appear as a scene-stealing mist.

At this stage, the analysis of evidence seemed to indicate little that was unusual. The group feeling strange sensations could have related to the humidity of the area and the sense of claustrophobia often associated with thick woodland, especially woodland with no defined tracks. The experience of seeing a face in the woods, especially at such a distance, could easily have been an animal or nesting bird in the undergrowth. Consequently, the first fieldwork trip to the wood

A range of paranormal phenomena have been alleged – not just ghostly.

did not prove fruitful but, as is so often the case, several elements of the trip were placed in a more prominent context in the light of the group's second visit.

The Second Investigation

The infamous flooding of the summer of 2007 saw the wood waterlogged for some period of time, delaying the return visit of the PSI team until October 2007. Four investigators that comprised the first team spent the early evening at the site. One team member reported a sense of nausea and 'fuzziness' on entering the site. The same investigator had reported the same experience on the previous visit. This possibly indicates a sense of fulfillment of expectation. On approaching the animal cage, the team unexpectedly bumped into a man and his dog, hunting for local wildlife. Following this unexpected turn of events, investigators experienced a range of human presence oriented events. These included the sound of footsteps on undergrowth and the sense of someone being stood nearby. However, it must be noted the unexpected event of finding someone else in a private wood is likely to have had a powerful effect on the perception of the investigators. Any snapping of twigs caused by wildlife, or ambiguous feelings caused by being in a spooky woodland context, were attributed to the possibility of a person being present.

Shortly after the first team left the wood, the second five-person team arrived on site. During the course of the trip several explainable events were reported. One investigator – who was not present at the time of the first fieldwork trip – reported seeing movement of something white close to the ground. The description was similar to the face reported on the previous visit, and reinforces the idea of the movement being an animal or bird rather than a face. Another investigator on several occasions reported seeing, out of the corner of their eye, a dark figure-like shape standing near to them. Such reports are not uncommon in woodland areas when a spooky context is applied to the area. This is often attributed to the movement of trees and shadows caused by unfamiliar woodland as the localised lighting changes.

Perhaps the most unusual report made related to the reports of previous eyewitnesses at the site. The leader of the second team began by directing the team to the clearing – 50ft north north-east of the same gated entrance – where dizziness was reported on the previous occasion. The investigation team swept the entire zone within 50ft of the entrance and could find no clearing at all, just dense woodland. The team proceeded to follow the established instructions for reaching the animal cage, but they progressed through the narrow wood, from one side to the other and back again, without finding the animal cage or any of the distinguishing features within its vicinity. The lead investigator described the experience as being like walking around an entirely different location to the one visited several times previously.

One thing that is certain is that the team *were* in the same woodland, with the only gated entrance to the woodland providing a definite marker. Could the team have experienced the change in geography in the wood reported by the original eyewitnesses? Was it a coincidence that the dizziness experienced by independent investigators bears similarities to reports of time slips and altered reality? Probably. The most compelling explanation for the experiences remains that the team – and possibly the original eyewitnesses – simply lost their sense of direction, as is so easy to do in untouched woodland with so few reference points.

The investigations of the private woodland remain of great interest. Although the realities of certain experiences were left unsolved, it helps to underline the serious pitfalls of investigating uncontrollable sites like this woodland of past and present legend.

INVESTIGATION OF A PRIVATE HOME, LYDIARD MILLICENT

The Private Case Method

Private cases are frequently those cases of a family distressed by what is occurring within their own home, wishing to keep the research confidential and with the aim of addressing specific activity. In this particular case, the family were not overtly distressed, more curious about what they had been experiencing. Furthermore, as the family are due to have moved and the house to have been demolished by the time of publication, PSI felt it was ethically justifiable to print details with no names attached. Private cases generally are investigated very differently to the other cases you will have read about in this book so far.

At the first point of contact, the client is assigned a case lead and their lead is responsible for all liaison with the family, including follow-up support. Private cases are always the organisation's priority cases and are typically dealt with within days of the first contact being made by the client. A questionnaire is sent to the client to try and gather as much information as possible prior to witness interviews being conducted. The PSI private case co-ordinator (PPCC) has extensive experience of interviewing people in distress and of providing ongoing support in such cases. Arrangements are made with the client for the PPCC and a colleague to visit them at their home to conduct interviews. It is essential that the interviews are done on an individual basis so that witnesses do not influence one another in their reporting, and also in case they wish to share anything with the PPCC that they do not want other witnesses to know. While the PPCC is conducting interviews, their colleague will be with the other witnesses and will request a tour of the premises to facilitate any future investigation. It is important to note at this point that it is rare for an investigation to result from a private case. More often than not, the family just want somebody to talk to about their experiences or may wish to be directed to a more appropriate

Lydiard Millicent, just west of Swindon, is the setting for a private house 'haunting'.

organisation if, for example, they are seeking a spiritual resolution. If any children have been witness to phenomena the PPCC will not, despite being Criminal Record Bureau checked, interview anybody under the age of 16 without their parent or guardian being in attendance. At the end of the interviews, the client is asked to keep a phenomena diary, in which they are asked to document any activity that occurs and to include dates, times, the people present, what happened and any precursors to the phenomena. At this point, the PPCC and the client will discuss the most appropriate course of action to be taken and decide whether an investigation is to occur.

When investigating private cases it is rarely appropriate for the PSI team in its entirety to be in attendance. This is primarily due to the sensitive nature of such cases and the space restrictions which are often imposed. Unless the reported phenomena is centred on a specific individual, the family will be asked to vacate the premises at the time of the investigation so that a thorough study can be conducted. In addition, before being allowed to participate in a private case, investigators receive compulsory additional training which reinforces PSI's strong ethical commitments and outlines the methods that are used.

As with most cases, it is important that the way in which a private case is investigated reflects the phenomena that have been reported. Therefore, if no fluctuations in temperature have been identified then thermometers will not be utilised. If the phenomena reported is predominantly visual in nature, then more cameras than in a regular investigation would be deployed. Similarly, it is essential that PSI attempt to secure high ecological validity and, as such, will arrange to be in attendance at the time at which activity has been perceived. For example, if a figure is seen in the master bedroom at 10am each Wednesday, there is little point in the team being there at midnight on a Saturday. Through matching circumstances as rigorously as possible, the team give themselves the best chance of being able to provide answers to the client's questions.

PSI do not use private cases as a way of furthering their own research in regard to their longitudinal studies so, therefore, EVP experiments are not conducted and neither will any investigator's paranormal belief levels be measured or their perception of spookiness in regard to the context research. Similarly, investigators are asked not to report any psychic impressions which they may have, as PSI's scientific methodology must be core in the investigation and must not in any way, intentionally or not, exacerbate activity or the perception of activity.

After the investigation is conducted, a thorough report is submitted to the client with the team's suggestions for natural causes of the perceived activity and ongoing support is always offered.

Background to the Lydiard Millicent case

In December 2007, the PPCC received an e-mail from a gentleman living in the Lydiard Millicent area of Swindon seeking an investigation of his home as a result of what he, his wife and their child had experienced. A meeting was arranged for a few days later for the PPCC and a colleague to visit the family to find out more.

The clients had moved into their home a year earlier and activity had been experienced from within the first few weeks of their occupancy. However, the family were due to be vacating the house in early 2008 and wanted to try to identify the cause of the activity before their departure. The man's wife had had many experiences in the house and, indeed, had had several experiences that she believed to be paranormal in nature throughout her life. He too had had experiences in their current home and their young daughter (just over a year old) had also seemingly responded to the activity.

In order to keep the identity of the premises confidential, no site history is provided. However, there was little in the site history known to PSI that could in anyway shed further light on what was reported. There was a rumour, told to us by the client, that a young girl had been killed on the road outside the property but, after liaising with the police, this remains uncorroborated.

Analysing the Reported Phenomena

As already discussed, the purpose of the investigation was to attempt to understand what may have contributed towards the clients' experiences. As such, it was essential that those present at the investigation were fully aware of the phenomena reported so that the team could systematically consider each incident and advance theories as to its cause.

It is unnecessary for us to detail the investigation itself as the investigators were merely responding to what had already been reported and, through spending time in the house, attempting to glean a greater understanding of possible contributory factors. PSI instead considered each incident reported to us by the family and presented the possible cause as identified by the team.

In December 2006, the lady of the house was moving washing from the washing machine to the tumble drier in the utility room when she felt that she received a firm push on her chest that actually made her fall over backwards and hit her head. It is possible that this may have been physiological in nature. The heat and/or steam from the washing may have led the witness to become light-headed, accompanied by the crouching position, which could have contributed to dizziness. This light-headedness may have caused the witness to fall backwards and the knock to the head may have resulted in a misattribution of being shoved. A strong erroneous muscular spasm is another possibility.

The following incident occurred in February 2007 early one morning. The client was dozing in bed, after being up with her daughter in the night, when she heard a key in the front door and assumed her husband had returned home after forgetting something. The bedroom door then burst open and she saw two men stood in the doorway with balaclavas over their heads wearing jeans, trainers and possibly polo neck jumpers. They were described as being stocky and chunky and around 6ft tall. The men disappeared, seemingly behind the curtain, after the witness asked: 'What do you want?' After searching the house, she did not find the men and when the postman arrived moments later he said he had not seen anyone. This report may have been a result of hypnopompic imagery. The hypnopompic state accompanies the process of awakening, when the individual is in a state of semi-consciousness. This state has been shown to contribute towards visual and auditory hallucinations. The PPCC also contacted the local police to ask if there had been any burglaries in the area at the time of the incident, matching the description of the account provided, but the police confirmed there had been no similar reports made so an actual attempted burglary is unlikely.

April 2007 saw the first apparent interaction with the child's toys. A toy on the toddler's cot has the ability to say different phrases to different tunes. In this occurrence the tune of *Row, Row, Row Your Boat* came on and a voice saying something to do with 'play' was heard over the tune. It was reported that the tune was not a tune programmed into the toy and the voice was blatantly different to the voice of the other phrases. Much time was invested by the team in trying to isolate the sound clips of *Row, Row, Row Your Boat* and a phrase about 'play'. These phrases were identified, but on two separate toys. *Row, Row, Row Your Boat* featured on a Cat & the Fiddle toy of the child's as one of the possible tracks, when pressing one of the buttons. The toy from the cot says 'time to play' when a certain part of the toy is activated. The witness report suggested that these sounds were heard simultaneously coming from the same toy in the nursery. The team were unable to manipulate the toys in such a way as to recreate the reported phenomenon. The possibility of memory conformity and memory contamination of the witnesses must be considered as a plausible explanation.

The presence of a child was first thought to be apparent in May 2007 when the client was sitting by the computer in the lounge and became aware that her daughter had stopped watching television and was looking at something in the doorway. As the client leant back in her chair to see what her daughter was looking at, she saw the outline of a figure which turned and walked towards the kitchen. This figure was subsequently seen by the client several times in the doorway to the lounge and was described as being a little girl aged 6-7 years with a 1960s hairstyle including a bow. She was reported as wearing an orange frilly dress, white socks and black shoes. The client felt her name may have been Patricia and that the girl was somehow unable to enter the lounge. This account remains of great interest to the team, in light of the repeated nature of the phenomenon. Unfortunately the reported apparition was not seen by team members or captured on video. One possible, but unlikely, explanation could be primed expectation as a result of the rumour of a girl being killed outside the property. PSI accepts that this is doubtful but it is provided as a possibility.

There was further activity centred on the child's toys. As the clients were sitting in the lounge, their daughter's rocking horse turned itself on and sang the words 'I'm a little pony.' However, PSI were informed that in order for the rocking horse to be activated, the ear needs to be squeezed. The team did not witness the rocking horse being activated of its own accord, but would suggest that a malfunction may have been the cause. It is possible that the ear could have been depressed earlier in the day and may have become naturally unstuck at the time at which it was reported to activate.

Interference with the plumbing was also reported. The taps in the kitchen were turned on to a normal stream seemingly of their own accord. Later that same day, the shower turned on, again, seemingly of its own accord. It must be noted that the shower was rarely used due to the family preferring baths, and the controller was very difficult to turn. A similar report on the same road had also recently been reported to the team, so it is possible that it may have been caused by a problem with the plumbing or a sudden change in water pressure that could have bypassed the need to turn the knob.

In August 2007 the client was in bed reading when the bedroom burst open. She reported seeing a black shape – around 5ft 9-10in tall – that she sensed was male but featureless. The shape disappeared, again behind the curtain. The team were unable to identify a definite cause for this report but, as the witness was in a relaxed state and reading, the impact of the hypnagogic state should be considered. The hypnagogic state is the state that accompanies falling asleep and, during this time, auditory and visual hallucinations are possible.

Additionally, when her daughter was asleep in her crib, the client reported that she had seen a woman standing in the nursery looking over her daughter. The woman was described as being 5ft 4in tall, of normal build, wearing glasses, having short brown hair brushed back from her face and wearing a navy blue skirt with a wine coloured jumper. The client says she had a friendly face and looked like her daughter, and she also felt she might be her husband's deceased mother. This woman had also been seen by the client in her bedroom, watching her husband as he slept. This ongoing phenomenon remains of interest to the team but as no footage of the reported apparition has been caught or provided it is difficult to draw any firm conclusions.

In October 2007 the male client was in his computer room late at night and heard scratching on the window pane, followed by a bang. He looked outside for an explanation but there was nobody there and no trees or other flora nearby. After the team examined the exterior of the site, they concluded that the size of the window sill is large enough for a cat or other animal to attempt to land on it, which could have created the noise that was reported. The team are aware of another similar case in the Swindon area that was proven to be caused by a bird tapping the glass as a result of seeing its own reflection.

Both clients, plus another family member, had reported ongoing corner-of-eye movement predominantly in the bathroom area and by the lounge window, but also in the child's nursery. These incidents had all been reported to occur in the left field of vision; this type of phenomena is a very common report made and current academic research suggests it may be natural and neurological in nature. The swinging of the clock pendulum in the hall can also create the illusion of unnatural movement when light strikes it. In the kitchen area, a smear on the glass leading to the conservatory is eye-catching and can be perceived as seeing someone go past.

The clients reported that their bedroom is always very cold, even when additional heat sources are used. Due to the consistency of this perception, PSI concluded that the structure of the room is the most likely cause of this sensation. Three exterior walls and a very large window can all contribute towards a naturally low temperature.

The sensation of being watched when in the bathroom was reported by both clients. Investigators present at the site also reported a sense of unease in the bathroom and identified the style of the tiling as a possible cause. The repetitive circular pattern can distort perception and may induce a psychedelic state. The structure of the shower cubicle may also contribute towards a sense of vulnerability as you cannot see all the way around it, due to it having solid walls rather than glass or curtains. Furthermore, the position of the bathroom in the house may add to this sensation as when in the shower you would be aware that the rest of the house is straight ahead of you, leading all the way through to the front door.

Finally, as our female client was standing looking into the mirror in the hall she reported that she became aware of a dark shape behind her. This effect was recreated by an investigator. Positioning oneself at a particular angle causes one's own shadow to be cast behind, appearing larger and to the right. No other possible causes have been identified at this stage.

Conclusion

The team were successful in identifying potential causes for many of the eyewitness accounts provided. The team cannot conclusively prove that their suggestions are the definite cause of the reported phenomena but are confident that their proposals could be contributory factors to the incidents reported.

The understanding of anomalous phenomena is limited by our knowledge of science as a whole. As the discipline develops, and our understanding of the human mind also progresses, a greater comprehension will be gained of the causes of anomalous experience.

In concluding this chapter, the PSI private case co-ordinator would like to extend the organisation's gratitude to the clients for their complete co-operation during the research and for their permission to include their case in this book.

The Swindon Arts Centre stands on Old Town's Devizes Road. Devizes Road was one of the oldest four main streets to comprise the old quarter of the settlement, which dates back to the Domesday Book of 1086.

In 1774 an orchard was sited on the area now occupied by the arts centre. In 1891 the recorded usage had changed to comprise one shop, a house and stables and four cottages. In 1892 the area was owned by solicitor Edward Goddard Bradford, presumably related to the Goddards who were, at the time, lords of the manor of Swindon. After the owners had moved to the city of Bath, the site was redeveloped into Bradford Hall, a public hall named after the family. Bradford Hall became a dance hall after World War One, and dances were staged there up until 1955. Meanwhile the Swindon and District Amateur Theatre Guild had moved between rooms above the former McIlroys store in the town centre and rooms in the Regent Street Methodist Hall. In 1955 Bradford Hall was converted into a theatre and arts centre before opening in 1956. Until 1994 the theatre was primarily used for amateur groups but has since extended to include a professional programme.

To this day the arts centre claims to have a resident ghost by the name of 'Mrs B'. Unusually, the nearby former Peg's Pantry and the slightly more distant Victoria Hospital have also claimed the Mrs B. figure as their resident ghost. She is said to be a lady dressed in brown that has been sighted in the seats at the rear of the auditorium, in the gallery bar and on the stairs. Staff members claim that lights have been switched on following them being turned off. Staff also claim to have seen fire doors opening and closing, seemingly of their own accord. Footsteps have also been heard in the apparently empty building and witnesses have reported feeling a presence. Various accounts

were made during recent renovation work, which include bricks being moved, batteries draining and a figure being seen. One former manager described the hooded Mrs B. being seen one evening on the right staircase. Ironically the staff were said to notice that none of the customers had used that side for the whole of that particular night.

In 1992, staff of the centre recounted further stories to the local newspaper, then the *Evening Advertiser*. One staff member recalled that she had passed a figure in the corridor, later realising she was the only person present on site. The member of staff further recalled:

'There are four different phone numbers in this building and one night they were all ringing simultaneously. Every

The Old Town's Arts Centre.

Formerly Bradford Hall.

time we picked one up, there was an open line, but no one was there. Then, one night, as I was going into wardrobe, my dog who was with me started barking and would not walk in there. Later, when we went back with someone else she went in fine, as if nothing had happened.'

It is fairly common, in haunting stories, for unexplained events to be essentially blamed on a historical figure. Whether or not a link exists, supposed paranormal activity at a particular site will always be associated with a researched historical figure.

The arts centre has drawn the conclusion that Mrs B., as the staff named her, was a daughter of the Bradford family. She is said to have been buried at Christchurch before the family moved to Bristol. The centre claims that the grandson of the gardener, who was paid a retainer to tend to the grave, backed up this assertion. The centre has asserted that, while little activity is reported on an ongoing basis, Mrs B. begins to make her presence known when the building is under some form of threat.

The centre seems to follow the general convention that theatres house ghosts. In fact it is difficult to find a theatre, of more than a century standing, that does not claim to have a haunting. One possible reason for this is the generally accepted superstitious character of many theatrical actors and theatrical superstitions, including the idea that all theatres should be closed for one night a week to allow ghosts an opportunity to perform plays of their own. There is also the tradition that a light should always be left on in an empty theatre. The various ghost-related reasons for this superstition are to ward off ghosts or to allow ghosts enough light to see, so as not to anger them and face the consequences.

Whether the ghost of the Swindon Arts Centre is simply a mandatory superstition or something more, might never be known. The centre proudly discusses its ghost on its website but, unfortunately, is not keen for the matter to be investigated.

The former Victoria Hospital on Okus Road in Old Town is the setting for Swindon's very few old-fashioned ghost stories.

Construction of the Victoria Hospital began in 1887 in the golden jubilee year of Queen Victoria. The hospital was designed by W.H. Read and was free, supported by voluntary

Victoria Hospital served the town from 1887 until 2007.

subscriptions. When it opened, the hospital cost £1,960 and had only six beds. Before its opening the nearest general hospital, serving the then 25,000 population of Swindon, was as far away as Purton. Victoria's role as a general hospital declined after 1959 when the Princess Margaret Hospital was opened further along Okus Road. Now the designated use for the former hospital is for residential development. The building is set among Victorian and Edwardian family housing, and has been officially designated by Swindon Borough Council as a building of significant local importance.

Swindon's few ghost stories should be indulged without prejudice and this account is no exception. It has been told, by folkloric tradition, by a friend of a friend. After the end of World War Two, one of the sisters of the hospital was going about her nightly business. The sister needed to cut through the theatre in order to reach another area of the hospital. As she reached the door to the theatre she found that a soldier in uniform, carrying a gun, was blocking her path. Eventually the sister resolved to use a different route and passed by the theatre. She noticed the soldier had disappeared and that a loose fitting had fallen on the other side of the door, which could have killed her had she walked that way. No one else on site knew of a solider in the building. This story is similar to many other ghost stories and the idea of a ghost appearing and averting a life-threatening disaster is a thread running through many ghost stories.

A further account arose from a sister who would regularly visit the former Peg's Pantry café on Devizes Road. The sister described a brown, hooded, young female figure that would sit on the hospital beds and then disappear. She reported that an impression would be left on the bed for a few seconds after she departed. The sister drew the conclusion that the apparition was the same ghost that roamed Peg's Pantry and the arts centre. Recent accounts have been reported by site security guards who have witnessed various phenomena in the now empty building. It must be noted that the Victoria Hospital was in use by the Primary Care Trust until the end of 2007 and the previous anecdote was only included in this book because authors knew the hospital would not be used for healthcare by the time of the publication of the book.

Ghost accounts of this nature are essentially stories and tend to correlate with any current activity within a location. However PSI strongly believe that treatment of ghost accounts in locations used by vulnerable people must be treated with the highest ethical regard; even though the story mentioned above is historical, and possibly semi-fictional, there is still potential harm to be done by releasing the story when the hospital is still occupied.

Other ghost accounts connected with disused care establishments in the town include the Princess Margaret Hospital (PMH), also on Okus Road. It was the district's primary hospital from 1960 until 2002, when all departments were transferred to the new Great Western Hospital (GWH) on the outskirts of town. Many strange rumours have been circulated by the former staff of PMH for a number of years. One such tale, in a geriatric ward, was of an old Scottish patient who threatened he would haunt them. The old lady who occupied the room after him was apparently heard to shout, with regards to a man supposedly sat in a chair, 'will you get that Scottish git out of this room?'

Another account relates to a former care home based in the Broadgreen area of Swindon town centre. One story tells of a lady who used to pull tea towels off the shoulders of staff when she was resident there. Staff reported that when she was no longer at the home tea towels would still, unaccountably, be pulled off their shoulders. Former staff also reported unusual mobile phone activity, being shoved on the stairs and seeing shadow-like figures.

CASE: PEG'S PANTRY, OLD TOWN   TYPE: HISTORIC, ONGOING

Another victim of the famed Mrs B. of the Swindon Arts Centre is the building that was once the nearby Peg's Pantry café. The site was once two linked cottages and, in the 1960s, part of an automobile garage. The one-time owner of the café and later Greek restaurant recounted the various experiences she attributed as being paranormal between 1978 and 1988:

'The first occasion where I noticed anything unusual was with a lady who was working for me; it was in the afternoon; closed after dinner, doing preparation for the afternoon. We were standing at the kitchen sink, which looked out onto the back yard. My colleague exclaimed that somebody had just come to the back door. I said there couldn't be; the yard was entirely blocked off at the time and there was no way in. She maintained that someone had passed the window. We went to the back door and, of course, no one was there. Apparently the figure was dressed in a dark hooded raincoat. We laughed it off at the time, thinking she'd just been seeing things. However, a day or two later exactly the same thing happened. Again we went out, and no one was there.

'After that things really started happening! Sometimes we would hear footsteps in the café after closing time. There would often be more than one of us, we would check the building and there would be no one there. We'd both hear them, and they were clearly footsteps rather than just random knocks. It got to the stage of being so frequent that I used to call out "Stop it! Behave and get yourself a cup of tea!" We used to call it "our ghost".'

As if this were not enough, the mystery seemed to deepen. The owner continued:

'At one time the caretaker of the arts centre used to be a regular customer of ours. One day we told him all about "our ghost", all the details, and he stopped still. He said he would stay exactly where he was, but that we were to go over to the arts centre and ask the manager about their ghost. I went to see the manager and he said their ghost was called Mrs B., a youngish person, wearing a dark cloak robe with a hood. I laughed and told him that we'd seen her too! I felt that she was not mischievous, but that she just does not like to leave the place. Funnily enough, one day a sister from Victoria Hospital came in for lunch. We told her about "our ghost" and she said that they had the same ghost down at the hospital.'

Peg's Pantry used to be on Devizes Road – the current building location is withheld.

The owner described another series of unusual events at Peg's Pantry:

'We went to the cash and carry one day and we bought a lot of bread for the café. It was quite busy in the café when we got back so we did not put it all away straight away. We put some of the bread on the kitchen work unit, but right at the back, against the wall. At lunchtime a regular customer poked her head through the door to the kitchen to say "hello" to me. Suddenly one loaf after another went 'whoosh' down onto the floor between us. She said "Did you see that?" and I responded that it would be the ghost. The bread could not have fallen, it was too far back on the surface.

'On occasion we would find that the cups had moved. We would leave the café tidy and ready to start the next day and we'd find the cups lifted and moved around, and my colleague would comment that we didn't leave them in that place. The ghost didn't like them where they were, but we weren't afraid. The ghost just seemed to be part of the place.

'We had a German Shepherd at one point. On Sunday we would take the dog in while we would give the café a good clean. We would try to get the dog to go through the door between the café and the kitchen, but it would not. After that we went through the shed into the back yard and tried to get the dog to go up the couple of steps into the kitchen but it still refused to go through.'

In many ways the Peg's Café case is the archetypal modern ghost tale. The presumed haunting began with a potentially natural event (seeing someone in a place they should not have been) followed by a series of possibly explicable events (noises, movement of objects, animals behaving strangely, etc) that are noticed in light of – or even because of – the initial perception of a haunting.

A fascinating aspect of this case is the chance to see a historical figure attribution in its infancy. Many streets or even wider areas are said to be comprised of buildings haunted by the same ghost; a local example is the monk of Highworth that is said to haunt High Street, Church, King and Queen public house and at least one private residence. Usually these supposed hauntings have been attributed to a historical figure long ago and it is difficult to tell where the story really started.

In the case of Peg's Pantry, the former owner can remember the moment when the attribution was made. In this case, and probably in many others, the attribution is somewhat suspect. The café workers described a woman in a hooded raincoat while the Swindon Arts Centre staff describe a woman in a brown hooded cloak. Consequently, the conclusion was reached that the figure was the same one and, for the decades that followed, it was assumed that Mrs B. haunted both locations.

Historical evidence suggests that the hill area of Swindon – now known as Old Town – contained Saxon settlements in the fifth to seventh centuries, and was recorded in the Domesday Book of 1086 as 'Suindune', roughly translated as 'pig hill'. Old Swindon or High Swindon, in more modern times, was a thriving market town. The Victorian era saw the creation of Swindon New Town and the two were incorporated as one municipal borough in 1900. Old Town is now one of the most picturesque and sought-after areas of the town.

From Tudor times to the early 20th century, Old Town's history was much entwined with that of the Goddard family. While the family were in evidence in Swindon before the 15th century, Thomas Goddard of Upham acquired the Manor in 1563 and his descendants were lords of Swindon manor until 1927.

The family manor house, also known as Swindon House, was set in the estate now known as the Lawns or Lawn Park. Swindon House was rebuilt in 1770, probably over an existing mediaeval building. The house remained empty from 1927 until World War Two, when it was occupied by British and US Forces. By 1952 Swindon House, or Lawn House as it was then known, was derelict and was demolished. Adjacent to the house was Holy Rood Church, which was the parish church of Swindon from 1154 until 1852. The church is still standing today and is under private ownership. Lawn Park, including the foundations of the house, are now under the management of Swindon Borough Council and are designated for public use.

The historical accounts of ghost sightings in Lawn Park start with soldiers stationed in the house in World War Two. The park contains a pet cemetery where the Goddard family erected headstones to each one of the family pets. It is rumoured that American troops using the park gradually demolished the headstones and local legend reports that a spectral white figure of Lady Goddard was seen to walk through the woods of Lawn Park. Apparently angered by the disrespect to the graves of her pets, the figure in white was said to terrify the young soldiers. In 1997 the *Evening Advertiser* reported the mystery of freshly cut flowers being regularly left on the remaining headstone, although the tender of the grave was never discovered. Reports of unaccountable unusual feelings and sightings are still occasionally reported in the wood area.

Lawn Park is one of the more traditional cases in a Swindon that is largely devoid of the folkloric white, grey, green or blue ladies that are in abundance in other areas of the country. These sightings are very much out-of-fashion these days, but do form an integral part of England's ghost folklore.

There is an account in *Morris's Swindon 50 Years Ago*, penned in 1885, that recounts a story of a pond beside a church, next to a mansion in Swindon. While the site is not named, considering the town boundaries at the time it seems entirely plausible, although not certain, that the tale relates to Lawn Park. The pond, which was filled in by 1885, was said to contain a door that led to a passage to the house. It was said that the tunnel was sealed as the 'laying place' of several spirits. A brave servant unblocked the door and opened the door a crack and saw several ghosts smoking pipes. They proceeded to transform into blue smoke and seep through the door.

After obtaining permission from the Borough Council and informing the police, the PSI team conducted a fieldwork investigation at the site in June 2007. The team were startled, having only just entered the park, to come face-to-face with a bearded Tudor man and a frilled wench. In fact at least a dozen Henry VIII figures and wenches were seen departing from a mediaeval-style banquet before the poorly-timed fieldwork could commence.

The church in Lawn Park was once Swindon's main church.

Lawn Park and Wood – formerly the heart of the Goddard Estate – has been the subject of ghost tales during the 19th century, World War Two and the 20th century.

Close to the foundations of what was once the impressive Lawn House.

Little time was spent at the foundations of the old manor house, the chosen place for the players of the Old Town Festival to camp, so the team concentrated on the wooded areas and the lake. Virtually nothing was experienced on site.

On the face of it, it would seem that the ghosts of Lawn Park are just the stuff of folklore, with modern sightings concentrating on the natural creepy atmosphere of woods at night.

Case: The Clifton, Old Town   Type: Folklore, historical

Most books of ghost accounts in Britain skip neatly over Swindon. Even books specifically written on the subject of Wiltshire hauntings nearly miss out the town, which comprises one third of the county's population. Where gazetteers of ghosts do mention the town, it is usually restricted to Lydiard House, with a poorly documented side-note about the hauntings of the Clifton.

Records of the origin of the Clifton site are often patchy. The Clifton's own website claims it was supposedly built on the site of a local priory, but no records to support this have yet been unearthed. An early documented legend tells of rumours that a graveyard was buried by a landslide. It is possible the priory story derived from this older legend. Before the pub's construction in 1878 the land was said to farm cypress trees, leading to the area being called Cyprus. Behind what is now the pub's car park there is an apparent cliff, created by the excavations of stone used for embankments along the Great Western line.

The Clifton itself is set on a residential street of Victorian terraces. This area was built from the 1870s to help house the railway-working population of the rapidly expanding Swindon. In keeping with the railway theme, the then hotel was named the Clifton Hotel as a tribute to the Clifton Suspension Bridge in Bristol, designed by Isambard Kingdom Brunel – the man who helped to bring the railway works to the town. The exterior of the pub still boasts a tiled mural of the bridge.

The pub has laid claim to at least four periods of documented haunting. The first is the traditional folkloric tale of a spectral nun. Legend tells that the nun walks the building at night. She is seen most frequently in one of the upstairs bedrooms but has also been sighted in the cellar and in the bar area. Modern sightings of the nun are infrequent; spectral religious figures do seem to have been out-of-fashion for a good number of years.

Haunting sightings where ghosts apparently continue to walk the routes they might have used in life – non-sentient, unaware of their surroundings or the people currently living in a building – are often tagged as being consistent with the stone tape theory, where the actions of a person long-passed are imprinted into the very fabric of a building, or area, and then replayed like a video tape for eternity.

The Clifton on Clifton Street.

The Clifton was named after one of Brunel's achievements.

This is a nonsense theory. Researchers often use models to try to explain something observable, but all too often they have no grounding in reality. The stone tape theory itself is drawn from a BBC TV play of the same name, which proposes this theory in an entirely fictional context.

Non-sentient figures are not the only activity associated with the Clifton, however. Several sources cite two periods of brief and intense poltergeist activity, once in the 1970s and once in the 1980s. The 1980s accounts are not well-documented, but the 1970s incident involves the apparently deliberate moving of glasses by unknown forces. It is said that, on two consecutive nights, a sherry glass seemingly rose from the shelf behind the bar and fell to the ground without actually breaking. The landlords in the 1970s also recalled stories of an earlier tale of a window that jammed for years. A landlord found the window opened one day. He shut the window and, apparently, the window would never open again.

In 2005 the then owners of the site reported seeing figures in the darkened cellar. On 5 March 2005 the Paranormal Site Investigators spent the night at the Clifton. Not unusually, the paranormal investigation revealed virtually no evidence. The landlady summed the case up perfectly by saying: 'We did hear a few unexplained bangs, but you get that in old buildings.'

Case: Cheney Manor & Old Town Co-op   Type: Current, ongoing

The Co-operative stores in Cheney Manor and in Old Town are the site for our next apparent hauntings. Numerous staff in the Cheney Manor store have reported odd experiences over many years. Most of the incidences seem to centre on the store-room, which is in the old part of the store built before it was expanded in the late 1990s.

One employee of the store, who has worked there for over 20 years, recounted her experiences:

'People have always experienced things here as long as I have worked here. Everything that happened to me has been in the day time. We do not know what is here but we always call it "Fred". Just before Christmas 2007, before the store had opened, another staff member and myself were walking through the warehouse and we thought someone had left the store music on because we could hear quite loud voices. We discovered no one had left music on and we couldn't really make out what they were saying, like they were mumbling.'

Another member of staff reported her experiences, again in the warehouse and staff area of the store:

'Frequently when I would walk out of the staff-room the kettle would seem to turn itself on. People would always blame me for setting the kettle off as whenever I left the room it would always seem to turn itself on. We did wonder if was just the kettle, but we changed the kettle and the same thing happened.

'On other occasions I've felt a chill and felt as if someone is standing behind me. Sometimes I've heard a voice like a whisper and turned around to find out who has been talking to me, but no one has been there.

'Things also seem to happen to new people when they start working here. Almost like whatever is here is letting them know he's around. Sometimes when I'm locking up at night and have turned the lights off I hurry to get out as I feel as if there is someone still there.'

The new aspect of the allegedly haunted Cheney Manor Co-op store.

Another member of staff described some strange events at the store:

'On one occasion someone felt a screwed up piece of paper thrown and hit them on the head. But there was no one else in the warehouse at that time. A male member of staff also told us about occasions when the warehouse was empty and the door from the warehouse to the staff room corridor would unaccountably slam shut. It was also reported that on occasion stock would fall off the shelves on the shop floor without any apparent explanation.'

Another long-standing staff member told us about her various experiences over recent weeks and months:

'Last week I was walking from the staff room onto the shop floor and I heard a girl's voice behind me calling 'mum'. As a mother whose daughter worked at the store I automatically turned around and said 'yes'. There was no one behind me. I immediately went to find my daughter, who was across the other side of the store.

'A couple of months ago I was in the warehouse with another member of staff and I remember being definitely tapped on the shoulder. I looked around to see what she wanted but she was stood about five feet away from me, where she couldn't have reached, and she said she had not touched me.

'In the middle of last year I was working on the shop floor in the mid-morning. I felt someone very definitely touching me on the back of my neck. I kept turning around but there was no one there. The next day someone seemed to touch me on the back of my head.'

Cheney Manor is not the only Swindon Co-op store to report odd happenings. At the Co-op store on the high street in Old Town there have been reports of a similar alleged ghost occurrence. On one occasion a Co-op staff member saw a figure of a man walking on the upper staff floors. He assumed it was the manager, as he was the only person up there, but then the manager emerged from a ground-floor door. On investigation, it was found there was no one on that floor. Several other staff members had apparently experienced something similar.

CASE: FORMER CINEMA, TOWN CENTRE   TYPE: FOLKLORE, HISTORICAL

Some accounts of hauntings are well-documented and publicised, while others bubble beneath the surface for many years before revealing all. The latter is very much the case with the cinema, now a pub, in Swindon's Regent Street.

Regent Street, as one of the main streets of the new town's shopping district, has contained the town's cinemas since the 19th century; the site was adjacent to the then hamlet of Eastcott and associated farmland. The small cinema that is now occupied by the Savoy pub was opened in 1937; a hotel formerly occupied the site. The building was the town's primary cinema until its closure in 1991, making way for modern multiplexes on brownfield sites. The old cinema was bought by JD Wetherspoons and opened as the Savoy in 1996, as it remains to this day.

Little was publicly known of the old cinema's haunting until the month the Savoy pub opened in 1996. A local man, who made a hobby of photographing old cinemas, shot an unusual photograph and sent it to the local newspaper. The image was one of a bearded man. The man told the newspaper that no one was present when he took the photo, claiming he was the only person in the building. The newspaper's own photographer confirmed the image had not been tampered with and could not find a natural explanation. The man told the newspaper: 'I didn't really believe in ghosts until now. Perhaps my outlook will be more open now. I've been taking photographs for 10 years and this is the first time that anything like this has happened.'

The man had reportedly taken 1,500 photographs of the site. As the original photograph is no longer available it is difficult to draw conclusions. However, the budding photographer may have come across the same problem as many investigators of the paranormal. Chance problems with cameras seem to be fairly uncommon, especially before the introduction of digital photography, but, when taking over 1,000 photographs, the law of averages states that it is quite likely that one photograph will contain something unusual but quite natural.

This pub was once the town's main cinema.

Ghost researchers frequently report that a single unusual photograph can trigger a whole haunting case, as anything unusual noticed after the photograph is blamed on the supposed ghost. This case was quite the reverse: the publication of the photograph in the *Evening Advertiser* sparked a media-led exposé of hauntings experienced over previous decades of the cinema's operation.

A handyman reported one recent account, in the latter days of the cinema, from 1987 to 1991. He told the newspaper: 'I never saw anything but heard footsteps walking across the foyer and projection box. One Sunday I was there and heard the door click and footsteps walk across but there was no one there.'

A few days later a former projectionist of 25 years standing came forward to discuss his ghost experiences with the newspaper: 'I would be sitting in the rest room upstairs when I would hear someone open the door of the projection room, walk through to the rewind room and put a spool on. I would go out to see who it was and there was no one there.'

Later that month, another former employee approached the *Evening Advertiser* with his experiences.

'My first encounter came one Sunday afternoon when I was alone in the cinema. I had been sitting in the back row of Cinema One listening to some music and decided to walk round the auditorium checking the lighting. When I reached the front I glanced towards the back, where to my surprise I saw a man standing directly behind the seat where I had been sitting. We stood there intently watching each other for some seconds and I was on the verge of calling out to ask who was there. But in the end I just ran off and then crept back up there an hour later but it had gone.'

The media campaign concluded that the ghost, named George, was a former projectionist for the cinema who had died in an accident. Despite research at the time, no evidence could be found of such a person working at the cinema.

The Health Hydro (otherwise known as Milton Road Baths) is run by Swindon Borough Council and currently offers a wide range of leisure and health facilities including swimming pools, gymnasium, Turkish baths, a natural health clinic (opened in 1987), and meeting rooms.

The 1889 Ordnance Survey map (1:10,560) shows the site as open land, possibly small fields, a market garden or a park. There were open fields to the south-east, and it was otherwise surrounded by residential development. The building opened in 1891 or 1892, and housed two swimming pools, Turkish baths, washing baths, a suite of medical consulting rooms and a dispensary.

The Health Hydro was designed to supply health care to members of the Great Western Railway (and their families) via its Medical Fund Society. The society had been set up in 1847 in response to pressure from workers who suffered industrial injuries and whose communities had been ravaged by illness, and the site was built to answer the growing needs of society members, by supplementing facilities already provided elsewhere. The society based its headquarters at the site and it continued to own the premises until 1987 when, under threat from developers, the site was bought by the then Thamesdown Borough Council as a community health facility.

For years the Victorian building has reputedly been stalked by a ghost called Arthur who apparently walks the corridors at night and moves papers around; he was assumed to be the companion of a nameless woman who is rumoured to speak to unwitting people in the building.

One member of staff in 1991 remembers an encounter with the ghost. He claimed he was locking up the building when he heard a polite female voice from behind a door saying 'what are you doing here?' He told the local newspaper: 'You know when a cold shiver runs up your spine? Well that's what happened to me. I was not overly keen to meet her. A muffled voice said something again but I didn't catch it. I didn't want to hang around to find out what was going on.'

The former Victorian Turkish Baths.

Ghost tales hit the press not long after the modern baths opened.

Other experiences reported from this time include strange knocks on doors, unusual creaks and footsteps, lights being switched on when there was no one in the building and doors opening and closing of their own accord. Staff felt the ghost dated back to World War Two when, as during World War One, the building was used as a hospital. The drained pool was used for patients and what is now the women's changing room and Turkish bath suite was thought to have been a morgue. The Turkish baths boasted stained-glass windows, more than one of which in the ladies' baths featured a five-pointed star suspended above a crescent – an emblem familiar to modern Wiccans interested in the feminine mysteries. It must be noted that this design element does not necessarily indicate that pagan iconography was deliberately incorporated into the architecture; in fact, the design probably refers to the components of the Turkish flag.

In the early 1990s the staff of the baths came attributed Arthur to a figure from a historical picture of the baths from the 1930s. The local newspaper, then the *Evening Advertiser*, obliged by printing the picture. By the following week a reader had unearthed a better quality version of the photograph, which actually showed the 'ghost Arthur' to be a live woman!

The photograph saga continued until more recent times, however, as one woman described:

'I used to swim at the baths every day, early morning and evening, as I was in a local team. I was walking down one of the corridors on my own once through the door across from the reception where there is a large picture on the wall and a little old man used to be in the picture some days and other days he was missing. I told my team friends and we looked at it together on more than one occasion and they saw the same as me. He was rumoured to walk around the baths but I never knew why he was there, although over the years Milton Road Baths has been many things.'

PSI are due to investigate the Health Hydro in 2008 and hope to find out enough to assess the claims that the ghost Arthur still walks the building.

Case: Public House, Town Centre   Type: Current, ongoing

Twelfth Hour Investigations had been conducting investigations into claims of hauntings, ghostly sightings and strange occurrences across the county of Wiltshire and its surrounding areas for just over a year and a half when they were told about the public house situated in the centre of Swindon. The stories told of a historic building that was supposedly haunted by two different spirits.

The first, and more commonly reported, is that of a dark figure that has apparently been seen moving around on the ground floor in the seating area of the public bar. This mysterious apparition has been reported by many who claim to have seen it out of the corner of their eye yet, on inspection, that strange figure is never around. This shadowy figure has also been seen standing outside the door at the back of the pub, which leads out onto a wooden walkway with a scenic view of the stream that runs past the building.

The staff and owners at the location also reported that they saw a lady enter the bar area and walk up the stairs that led to the restaurant on the second floor. Thinking her to be a customer, one member of staff followed her up shortly afterwards to take an order from her, only to find nobody on the upper floor. The only way up to, and down from, the restaurant is the one staircase that is situated next to the bar area, but the people who witnessed the lady walking up the stairs claim they did not see her come back down at any time. The rumour, from a supposed medium who visited the pub, claims that the lady used to work in the building when it was a mill and lived in accommodation close to the land that the mill was built on. According to the mystic, the lady's young son had suffered a fatal blow to the head in an industrial accident that she felt she had caused and, according to the medium, this was why the lady visited the upstairs area of the building – because this was where the accident happened, and she felt guilty for what she had done. This sounds like an interesting yet slightly macabre story but on further inspection there are no records of such an accident occurring.

An investigation that was conducted into the supposed haunting of the location did not provide any proof of the activity that had been reported (i.e. the sightings). The team members present on the night conducted numerous vigils on both the upper floor and lower floors of the building. However, two people present reported hearing a voice in the ladies' toilets on separate occasions during a team break, yet neither knew the other had witnessed what they had. The first team member exited the toilets and immediately told a fellow teammate what they had heard and, as they were talking, a second team member exited the ladies toilets and reported they had just heard and received a shocked reception. Twelfth Hour were unable to recreate or explain but, in retrospect, the team wonder if the mumbling noise might have been caused by plumbing or outside noise.

The only other occurrence witnessed on the night Twelfth Hour spent at the location was the visual oddity witnessed by all members present. It consisted of large white flashes that appeared randomly on the wall opposite the top of the stairway that leads from the bar up to the restaurant area. After trying to recreate this, the team were unable to produce anything like it but it was soon realised to be light from cars passing outside, shining through the windows high up on the walls on the opposite side of the room. Due to the distance that the team were from the road, they were unable to hear the cars at the time they passed and cast light into the room.

If Swindon is known for anything, it is probably for its railway works. 1835 saw Parliament approve the construction of a railway line between London and Bristol, appointing Isambard Kingdom Brunel as its chief engineer. In 1840 Daniel Gooch suggested Swindon as an ideal location for the Great Western Railway's depot and works. As noted elsewhere, the citing of the works transformed Swindon from a 'small hill-top market town' into a quickly expanding railway town. By 1851 the works were employing 2,000 men and churning out a train per week. By 1900 the works were employing three-quarters of the town's population. In 1962 Swindon stopped building new locomotives and the works declined, finally closing in 1986.

Much of the old site was regenerated to become the Designer Outlet Village. The engineer's office is now the headquarters of English Heritage, which also houses its National Monuments Records on site. Also on site is the new headquarters of the National Trust; the old pattern store became a bar and then restaurant. The STEAM railway museum and an industrial estate also occupy former railway buildings. There are still a number of disused buildings and areas on the old site. The UK Government proposed the whole area as a World Heritage Site.

It would be reasonable to judge that ghost stories arise from places people have connection with; often well-used, long-standing public buildings. There are certain types of premises which will always seem to have a ghost tale to tell. What is most surprising about the expansive Swindon railway works is that so few ghost stories are associated with the sites, either under their new or old uses. Several second-hand stories about the Designer Outlet Village being haunted have been told, leading to a general haunted reputation for the site, without anyone really seeming to know why.

Part of the proposed World Heritage site.

Employees in the various English Heritage former railway works buildings have described unusual experiences. Temporary night workers have reported that 'everyone' gets 'spooked' in the toilets and that an air freshener once fell off a wall. It was also reported by one worker that they often felt people were walking down the corridors towards their desk but there was never anybody there. Another account tells of an experience in the car-parking area around the English Heritage offices; one early evening a lady claimed to see a man walking across the car park and then clearly saw him walk though a wall. Additionally, in the downstairs ladies' toilet of what was the Pattern Store Bar, one customer reported seeing the figure of a man in his mid-fifties wearing traditional work clothes, chewing baccy with short hair swept over his head.

It seems fairly likely that there are various individual experiences that are undocumented or have not seen the light of day. It is interesting to note that two television programmes have been made about individual experiences in the English Heritage offices and the railway works generally. However, despite this likelihood of unearthed material – which equally applies to any location – the railway works seems to be one of the most unusually non-haunted areas of Swindon.

The PSI team investigated the site in 2008 but, as is so often the case, nothing to report was found.

Holmes Music has been operating from Faringdon Road since the 1970s, where the building was previously used as a shop for raincoats. The history of this Victorian-built area is considered in the census reports of both the adjacent Milton Road Baths and Railway Village (Bathampton Street).

The same family has run the shop since it moved to the site but, in the early 1990s, they started to notice some odd events which built quickly over a period of time. The first unusual activity noticed was by the mother, who claimed old one-penny pieces had started to appear, being flung out of apparently nowhere. The family began to wonder if she was imagining it until it started to happen to other people too. On the middle floor, above the shop, there was a low-hanging canopy that had been covering the ceiling for some time. At the time when the coins were apparently being flung around downstairs the canopy was taken down to reveal – to the surprise of all concerned – mounds of dusty old coins nestled on top of the canopy that came crashing down when the canopy was removed.

Activity seemingly escalated as small Allen keys, frequently used in the shop, were unaccountably flung at unsuspecting customers. On one occasion, when young children were upstairs watching television, a fire extinguisher was, by all accounts, thrown into the room. On another occasion the staff thought one of them was thundering down the staircase but soon realised that a step ladder, that was previously firmly fixed upstairs, had come tumbling down the staircase. For this short period of time workers also noticed an indefinable but extremely unpleasant smell first thing in the morning when opening the store.

Holmes music store on Faringdon Road.

Other odd events involved one of the working boys losing his wallet and discovering it, very prominently, in the middle of the office floor upon opening up the next working day. On another occasion a credit card was taken by a member of staff at the till and seemed to vanish on the spot, literally never to be found again.

The escalating activity prompted staff to call in local psychic investigators and what was then HTV, who filmed a segment about the incident. The investigators seemed to feel the activity was centred on the second floor of the building where they laid crystals, dowsed and tried to clear the building. Since that time staff have experienced little.

In recent months small and odd things have happened and the staff still blame the supposed ghost. Penny coins have also started to turn up unexpectedly, but not 'thrown' as they were reported to be before. Whether this is linked to the former haunting is not clear in the minds of the staff.

The memory of the events is so distant in the minds of those that had experiences, being recounted some 15 to 20 years later, that it is difficult to examine the circumstances closely enough to draw any conclusions about possible causes. The cessation of activity following visits by the psychic investigators is notable but it is possible that the psychological sense of closure would have been a factor. The PSI are discussing access with the owners to assess the more recent reports.

Case: Town Centre's Haunted Homes in the Press   Type: Various

Swindon seems to have a tradition of haunted-house occupants parading their problems to an eager mass media. Elsewhere we have presented the Penhill Drive and Melksham Close haunted houses, which were discussed at length by the local press in the 1960s. Since that time the local newspaper has presented several more from the town centre and Old Town area, namely Faringdon Road, Elmina Close, Quarry Road and one house, unusually, on an unnamed street.

On several occasions the press have been more than happy to print the exact address of such haunting cases, but there are no reproductions of house numbers or individual's names in this book. This is an ethically sensitive area and horror stories have been told of so-called paranormal researchers knocking on doors asking to see a decades-old ghost, sometimes once a new family has moved in.

On the flip side, is it worth questioning why individuals choose to confide their 'haunting' in the local press? A disproportionate amount appear to be in council housing where tenants have requested to be rehoused; it always remains a possibility that the involvement of the media is part of a rehousing campaign. Therefore, this section presents several cases in private or rented accommodation where motivations for involving the press are open to the imagination.

The first case is in Elmina Close; part of the 1880s Victorian-built Broadgreen area where homes were built largely to house the increasing railway-working population. In 1998 the local newspaper reported night-time terrors. The 27-year-old occupant recounted: 'My ex-girlfriend was staying over one night when she suddenly sat up in bed and started talking to someone. She said it was definitely a man and, although the figure was quite shadowy, she said she could see a Roman helmet. But I couldn't see anything.' Some weeks later the man had a house guest whom he claimed he had not relayed this story to. However, the guest asked if the home was haunted. 'He said he'd felt a cold presence in the room and he really believed there was someone in there with him. That was really spooky because I hadn't mentioned anything to him. That's when I started to think there might be something in it.'

Once they started to believe their house was haunted, the case, according to the paper, became exacerbated. The man's girlfriend was in bed at night when she became convinced a wardrobe would fall on top of her; at the same time she felt paralysed. Other house guests reported feeling a sense of presence and night-time paralysis. Sleep paralysis is a well-known natural phenomenon often related to haunting cases. The fact that other activity increased, following a recognition of the haunting, could point towards expectation of paranormal events.

Up the hill into Old Town's Quarry Road is the site of the second case. The road is so-called because it runs alongside the Victorian-built Town Gardens, which used to be the site of a great quarry. In 1977 an 83-year-old self-proclaimed psychic recounted his recent experiences to the local newspaper, which included words appearing across his living room wall and disappearing just as quickly:

'They did not make words or any sense. I am psychic. I have seen ghosts and I remember them vividly. I could draw them though they appeared to me many years ago. I am not at all scared but I am interested in what it can mean. It does seem likely that someone from beyond, or perhaps from another planet, is trying to communicate, but so far it is all a mystery.'

The night before this report, the man claimed a red light, in the shape of a cross, appeared floating in his bedroom. The previous week he had claimed his bedroom was filled with 'hundreds of old photographs, portraits of people from about the beginning of the century, fluttering in the air'.

One alleged haunting related to an undisclosed house on Quarry Road.

Clearly these events on Quarry Road could not be said to be misattribution and the man seemed to believe what he was reporting, although his motivations for involving the press are anyone's guess.

Back down the hill on Victorian Faringdon Road is the location of the following report, from 1987. The house's occupant felt a ghost was the cause of the smell of smoking cigarettes and a cold patch on the stairs. The occupant seemed to form some sort of impression of 'a tall bearded young man with unusually bony wrists'. A simple case of possible misattribution was leapt upon by the newspaper, which began searching for a dead person to blame the haunting upon. Perhaps not surprisingly, they succeeded in finding a deceased tenant:

'He was a very slim man with long hair. I remember he had been working as a driver, but when he stopped that he seemed to become depressed and a different person. He got thinner and thinner and I sometimes saw him with bandages on his wrists. He was always locked up in his room, and never said anything. But several tenants lived in the same bedsit as Lucienne before I sold the house in 1984. They never complained about any haunting, and I know nothing of this cold patch.'

Another witness recounted their memory of the deceased former tenant:

'I was cleaning out my fish tank to put my gerbils in, and he joked to me that they would drown. His body was found just over a week later. He was very much a loner and you hardly ever saw him. His body lay undiscovered for a week because nobody thought anything of not seeing him around. I am a bit sceptical about the cold patch because he never went up the stairs. As far as the odours go his bedsit certainly stank.'

The final brief report comes from 1977, about an unnamed council-house in the town centre. An anonymous but well-known local priest conducted an exorcism following complaints of an evil presence to the then Thamesdown Borough Council. The family was rehoused and the new tenants are happy, at present. A council spokesperson told the newspaper:

'The house is between 70 and 100 years old and there had been no previous reports of strange happenings. We are assured that the complaint was genuine. There was a strange feeling in the house, which reacted on the child, who became very disturbed. Apparently, there was some sort of evil presence there, but everything is all right now.'

At first this looks like an open and shut rehousing campaign, but there is some evidence of official collusion. In the first place this case is the only known account where the newspaper has not proudly announced the names and streets (if not house numbers) of everyone involved. This suggests a certain level of handling by officials as the newspaper clearly had the information prior to speaking to the official. It is also striking that the council seemed to treat other cases with a certain amount of distance, whereas in this case the council spokesperson even talks of being 'assured' of the genuineness of the 'complaint'. Furthermore, the article clearly stated that the exorcist was a *bona fide* priest.

What is mysterious about this case is why, seemingly, the local authority chose to involve the newspapers. Similarly, what made the council so convinced that this haunting was genuine? Confidentiality rules still apply so we may never know.

Stratton Road is the setting of an allegedly haunted private house. The house in question is a 1930s detached property on the road between the Magic Roundabout and the Greenbridge Retail Park. One inhabitant lived in the house from the late 1960s to the early 1970s and claimed the same unusual phenomenon was seen several times a week over the course of five years. She said there was 'something' in the garden and that everyone else saw it too. This is the story in her own words:

Stratton Road in central Swindon.

'The house was detached with land to the side of it. Anyone who knew us knew not to knock at the front door, but to walk round to the side of the house to the back door when calling. We fitted a kitchen window, which opened onto this side path around the house.

'We would actually see something walk past the window in the kitchen. First of all I kept seeing this happen when at home with children. As I was at home a lot with the children we used to have a lot of visitors. People would sometimes say to me "someone is coming". They would tell me that someone was coming past the window. I would think "who is that" and rush outside to see who was there, but no one was ever there. This used to happen four or five times a week, every single week over the course of the five years. It was not just to me; dozens of visitors to the house saw something through the window. The odd thing was that it never came around the corner to the back of the house, just round the side past the kitchen window.

'I didn't want to believe it myself, did not want to put the name "ghost" onto it. One day some friends came up and one of them was a "believer" in this sort of thing. One day we were washing up by the sink by the window. One of them said "you have a visitor". I replied that that was our "ghost"; the first time I'd ever used the word to describe it. That was the first time I'd told my husband.

'We also ran a small business from the house with three other staff. Unknown to me one day when they came to work my husband asked them if they'd ever seen the figure walking past the window. They said they had all seen it; I'd never discussed it with any of them.

'At the time when we were selling the house I was washing up one day and looking out of window. I saw "him" in full colour: he was fully solid and slightly stooped. A slightly thinning, bald head. I didn't totally see his face but he had a red jumper on, which made me think that it was my mother to begin with. I even went to our neighbour to describe the man and he said it matched the description of the father of the person who used to live in our house.

'Something similar also happened just the once at the garage down the road. We used to chat to them quite a bit. One year the garage shut early for Christmas and when the staff came back they came to us and asked if we'd heard what had happened. In the garage the lads had gone out the back to collect tyres. They went back to the boss and told him they weren't going back out there, as there was a ghost of a man stood out there. Their boss went crazy and told them to stop being stupid. When the boss went out back to investigate himself the man was still stood there. When we heard it we thought the garage was out for publicity and kept expecting to see it in the paper; but they never told anyone, just other people in the trade.

'I do know that the new people at the house have not experienced anything. But they have altered the house considerably since we were there, which could have something to do with it.'

While the Stratton Road case is not a dramatic haunting, it remains more interesting than most from a researcher's perspective. The occupant of the house was not a career experiencer – she did not make a habit of experiencing phenomena before or after living on Stratton Road – suggesting that it is not something innate to her psychological make-up. Similarly she reports that various people, who were unprimed, reported seeing the same thing. This adds some more validity to what was experienced, suggesting it was not just an internal mental event. However, the strong possibility remains that some unknown but natural factor caused the sightings. The mystery may go unsolved, as it would be deeply unethical to approach the current owners to examine the property.

Case: Bathampton Street, Railway Village   Type: Current, ongoing

The collection of Victorian houses known as the railway village, located adjacent to the town's shopping centre, was constructed in the 1840s. It has been proposed by the government to be part of the town's railway World Heritage Site.

The 1841 decision by the Great Western Railway Company to construct an engineering works 'some two miles from the hilltop market town of Swindon' meant that housing would quickly be needed in what was, at the time, open farmland. The railway village consisted of 280 two-storey cottages, as planned by Isambard Kingdom Brunel, built from locally mined stone. The model village was designed to be self-contained, including a church, vicarage, school, parks and swimming baths (now known as the Health Hydro). A decade later the Mechanics' Institution was built in its central square and the whole area is currently a conservation area of 'special architectural or historic interest, the character of which is desirable to preserve or enhance'.

Bathampton Street – an undisclosed house is the subject of current 'happenings'.

The railway village's Bathampton Street is the site of an alleged haunting that has spanned a generation. One of the family members involved recounted the story so far:

'Whatever it is sits on one of my brothers at night. It is really terrifying for him. My brother never has time off work but last Saturday he woke up twice with this thing sat on him; once at midnight and once at three in the morning. Couldn't get back to sleep and couldn't work the next day; he never normally has time off work. He was as white as a sheet when I visited him the next day. It's happened at least four times now and we really don't know what it is. It had also happened

The railway village was part of a proposed World Heritage Site.

to my other brother, it was sat on top of him like pure energy; he bit into it. He said it was like biting into a sponge. Years ago my sister, when she lived in that house, felt something sitting on her legs at night.

'At the same house I came to visit my father. As I entered the house I stood by the door and I could not believe what I saw. This was the first time I'd actually seen anything unusual. There were four black things on the wall. I was freezing from head to toe. I said prayers and demanded they go; people had told me to do this. My hair was really standing up. It was like in the film *Ghost*: the black things; horrible, really black. I'd never seen anything like that before in my life. I was just watching and praying for what seemed like ages. Maybe for a minute, or maybe longer.

'While I had never seen anything before I did experience something at another house. Something got into bed with me. Thinking it was my husband I asked 'Is that you?' As I touched it I went straight through its body and I couldn't breathe, I was left gasping for breath. Another night, at home, I was sleeping alone as my husband had gone fishing. As I woke something was slowly pulling the duvet right off me, until it was on the floor. About two months later I visited my daughter and the same thing happened. I started to wonder if it was something that I was carrying around with me. Back at the house on Bathampton Street, about six months ago, I entered the house and was at the bottom of the stairs. I felt someone go past me and looked round to see someone disappear, they were wearing a herringbone jacket or coat. I asked my father, in the next room, whether anyone had been through the room and he said no.

'One night my granddaughter was staying with us. When in bed she told us that her great gran – my mother who has passed away – was coming in to pick her up. When my husband turned on the light he saw hand print impressions on the duvet that were larger than our granddaughter's.

'A friend of mine used to do psychic work. They said this, whatever it is, came through the bathroom. It was all about the archway, she called it a funny name I can't recall.

'About six weeks ago we got a Roman Catholic priest to bless the house, and also my house. But it's still all carrying on.

'The things that happened to my sister happened around 25 years ago. It's been going on for years and years; although some years ago I lived there for four years and never experienced anything strange. Sometimes it goes quiet for months on end, but then it just starts up again. This all started before we lost our parents, so I don't think it's them. Ages ago my brothers thought it might have been our grandmother, but I don't think it's her.

'About three years ago someone told me there was a fire in the Bathampton Street house and that someone died. I don't know if that is true or not though.'

The Bathampton Street case is fairly unusual. Many hauntings can be boiled down to possible misattribution: natural but unexpected things taking place, or individual bias leading to the attachment of a haunted label to a building.

While many of the happenings of this case could clearly be naturally explainable – including the possibility of sleep paralysis, hypnogogic and hypnopompic imagery explaining the night-time perceptions – instances such as non-fleeting views of figures are less explainable. It should be considered that it is possible that psychological factors could be at play. However, it would not be ethical to draw any such conclusions. At the time of writing, the private case division of the Paranormal Site Investigators team is working with the family to try to help them understand what may be happening.

Council housing estates are anecdotally thought to produce more than their fair share of haunting cases, especially poltergeist cases; perhaps because of the psychological trauma sometimes thought to trigger such events, or even the benefit of hoaxing a case. Perhaps England's most famous haunted case was in a council-house: the Enfield poltergeist case, handled by the Society for Psychical Research from 1977. Another known council-house case is that of Melksham Close, Penhill, reported in 1985.

Much of the site on which Penhill was built was farmland and fields, historically located in the Stratton St Margaret parish, itself once a small village in the possession of the physician of William the Conqueror at the time of the writing of the Domesday Book in 1086. The parish has been subsumed by the urban mass of Swindon and several farm cottages are now located in the estate of Penhill.

The Penhill estate also contained one of the main wells used by Arkells Brewery, established in 1843, to draw water for its beer. It is bordered by possibly historic woodland that is now the park of Sevenfields Nature Reserve. The estate itself comprised over 2,500 houses and was built from 1951, at the same time as Parks and Walcot, partly to house overspill from London. Penhill remains in the bottom 10 per cent of the most socially deprived wards in England. The character of the estate differs from area to area, but Lower Penhill (known locally as the Valley, and containing Melksham Close) is known to be particularly socially deprived.

Poltergeist (from the German for 'noisy spirit') is a hypothetical construct; no one knows, scientifically, what a ghost is, but poltergeist is a term used to describe a haunting that fulfils certain characteristics. Poltergeist cases, therefore, tend to include cases where the haunting manifests as objects or people being moved by seemingly unknown forces.

Melksham Close in the area known locally as the Valley.

This label seems to fit the reports made by the Swindon local newspaper, then known as the *Evening Advertiser*, in August 1985. The tenant recounted two previous incidents of hauntings in her house in Melksham Close. Apparently one old man, who used to live at the house, dug a large question mark out of his front lawn. The 1985 occupant told the newspaper: 'Apparently he was being haunted and made the question mark as if to say: "why me?"' The newspaper also reports that the teenage couple, occupants of the house in 1980, fled the house 'after furniture was hurled across the room and door locks smashed'. Apparently the house was then blessed, but not exorcised.

The 1985 occupant of the house, a 22-year-old living with her 15-month-old son, told the newspaper that her fear of the poltergeist had led to near-exhaustion and a nervous rash. She said:

'In the past two weeks strange things have been happening. My bed was pushed from the middle of the room against a wall and I felt someone or something pulling at the back of my jumper. I have also heard tapping on the window of the back bedroom but whenever I go to take a look there is nothing there. I want to get out of here. I dare not go to bed until it gets light at about 5am.

'The neighbours are very sceptical and say I'm just making it up to get rehoused, but they don't have to live here. I want out before my nerves are completely shattered. I don't hold out much hope of the council acting quickly though.'

In an article two days later, the then Thamesdown Council – through its housing spokesperson Councillor Derique Montaut – gave its version of events:

'We cannot rule out any option. If we feel her distress is genuine and caused by a haunting we would consider bringing in a psychic expert to investigate the house. We could also ask one of our staff to stay in the house overnight. We would certainly rehouse her if the claims she has made turn out to be founded, but we are also aware that sometimes people use excuses like this to try and get quick transfers.

'Our inquiries have revealed that nobody has ever died in the house and the question mark in the garden was put there by a previous tenant who was asked to tidy up his garden. We feel it was just a mickey take at the council's expense.'

Councillor Montaut added: 'I don't believe in ghosts but we are concerned for our tenants' welfare and if [the tenant] is being caused genuine stress through living in that house we will do all we can to help her. These phenomena seem to happen at very irregular intervals, though, so it will be very hard to investigate properly.'

There are a lot of theories that seek to explain poltergeist cases. There is enough detail in the Melksham Close case to briefly consider these. One unscientific theory states that poltergeists are either mischievous or angry spirits. It is difficult to apply non-science to such a case, although it might be reasonable to conclude that, as the events are not attached to specific people – accounts were given by successive tenants – and no deaths took place at the house, this might not be a relevant explanation. Another theory states that poltergeists are agent-focused, meaning that the paranormal events revolve around one person. Often this is considered to be a pubescent child and the theory considers poltergeists not to be spirits, but to be the psychokinetic outward manifestation of psychological trauma. Again, as this case spans several different owners, it seems unlikely to have a single focus. Scientists have claimed that poltergeist activity can be caused by physical explanations, such as static electricity, electromagnetic fields

Penhill was built as a council estate.

and infrasound. However, it is fairly unlikely that such subtle environmental factors could cause such a pronounced effect as a bed being moved across a room. Other theories for poltergeists include hoax and self-delusion. The possibility of hoax is often credible in these cases; in this instance the council noted that it might be a possible ploy to be rehoused. Self-delusion also seems possible; the council also suggested that occupants might have been listening to too many local stories.

Such cases are highly complex and, without firm evidence, any explanations remain speculative. It would be unethical to approach the current occupants of the house to ask if the haunting has continued so, with no further reports, we can only assume that this case is closed.

Melksham Close is not the only street on the Penhill estate that has reported problems with hauntings. One house on Penhill Drive claims to have driven a family to being rehoused in 1966. Needless to say, the family recounted all the gory details to the local newspaper, then the *Evening Advertiser*. The mother reported:

'It's terribly nerve racking I can tell you. We want to get out of here as soon as possible. I saw the shadow of a man on the landing in the day time but I did not mention it to the family, because I did not want to frighten them. We were in the hall one day and saw a clothes brush swinging backwards and forwards on its hook. The other brush was absolutely still.'

Also reported were locked bedroom windows being found mysteriously opened, doors banging and other odd noises. The 29-year-old daughter of the house continued:

'I woke up early one morning and saw a shadow of a man on my bedroom wall. I have also seen strange lights on my bed and the wall, and noises in the house late at night. I dare not sleep in my own room. One night my brother came home and was pinned to the wall with fear. He was paralysed with fear. He screamed, woke me up and then I screamed and went into mum and dad. He was as white as a sheet and we had to give him some brandy. He does not dare to come into the house now for more than a short time.'

The haunting appeared to be so severe that the family's son moved out permanently. However, the father of the house claims not to have experienced anything of the haunting. He said 'I can't get a decent night's sleep here, and I am worried about the health of my wife and daughter. I know that my son will never set foot in his room again. I have seen nothing but I definitely sensed something one evening before my wife and daughter had mentioned it.'

The family took drastic action to try to solve the problem. They asked the then Swindon Town Council to investigate the case, called the police and threatened to involve the Ministry of Housing and Local Government of the time. The local vicar was approached by the press and offered to say prayers at the house if requested and, two weeks after the press announcement of the poltergesitic activity, the Swindon Corporation rehoused the family. The family reported that they were happy and settled in their new house.

Three months later the press reported that the house had been exorcised and that a new tenant had finally been found. They stated that several people had been shown around, told the history and had refused to move in. There were no reports of the new tenant experiencing any problems.

The recorded history of this case does not state who performed the exorcism, or give any details of the process. An exorcism is an ancient religious ceremony that involves evicting evil spiritual entities from a place or even a person. Unconfirmed sources suggest that the Anglican Church appoints one exorcist per diocese, usually a retired member of the clergy. In December 2007 the *Daily Mail* reported that new Catholic Pope Benedict XVI had ordered bishops of each diocese to set up exorcism squads, primarily to combat satanic possession caused by the Internet and rock music! In modern times it is said that a panel needs to consider the case and ensure that mental illness is not the real cause of the problem.

There is the possibility that the house was not, in fact, exorcised. Local newspapers are notoriously overworked and it is possible that the wrong terminology was used. The house may, instead, have been subjected to a spiritual clearance, a service more readily available, especially as there had already been a spiritualist associated with the case. Whether the cessation of the problem related to the exorcism is difficult to say. Sometimes hauntings can be caused by psychological, physiological or other factors relating to an individual rather than place. The fact that reported problems stopped may simply relate to the individual family having moved out.

One aspect of such cases that always remains suspicious is the request to be rehoused. It is something of a cliché in the field of paranormal investigation that council-house tenants might invent a haunting in order to be rehoused if they do not like their current location. Needless to say it would be unfair and unethical to speculate on any such claims in this case.

Penhill Drive was the setting for an alleged 1960s poltergeist case.

The latest offering from the Penhill estate relates to Hannington Close. One former resident got in touch with the *Haunted Swindon* team and recounted her experiences:

'Around four years ago I lived in a flat in Penhill, Hannington Close, I found the flat very weird indeed. For example on occasion I would wake up and hear a baby crying. At first I thought it was the neighbour, the child next door. However I found that when the neighbour had moved and the place was empty that the same thing would happen. I would still hear a baby crying late

Hannington Close is near to the other alleged haunting on Melksham Close.

at night. Also one morning as I was washing up in the kitchen I had an experience: seeing a tall man stood in the hallway looking at me. He looked very pale and was wearing old attire. He was there about three minutes in all and then he seemed to disappear.

'I also had an experience one evening when I got home from work: I came through the front door and locked the door behind me and then I went upstairs to run a bath. As I got into the bath the water turned colder. Almost straight away I turned the hot tap on so as to warm the water up more. The second I turned the tap on, the door to the bathroom was bashed three times! I quickly got out of the bath fearing that an intruder had got into my flat. I ran out of the bathroom to investigate but no one was there.

'On other occasions I would also hear footsteps around my flat at night as I was trying to get to sleep. Additionally the temperature in my flat would turn icy cold at times, even in the summer months.

'I would also hear voices and sometimes feel the spirit or spirits touching me on the head or back. I finally had had enough and gave up my tenancy after four years, as I feared for my own safety! I would never go back into that house in Hannington Close, Penhill, again!'

This case offers similar experiences to others in this book, which have been expanded on. However one striking feature of the case is its location – Penhill, again. Considering Penhill comprises around one 25th of the houses of the borough, it usually accounts for a high number of census reports. And when you consider the number of private house cases in isolation, Penhill suddenly looks like it contains the most haunted houses in the town. Of course the sample is not necessarily representative, but it still raises questions.

Several of the Penhill cases, as discussed elsewhere, did emerge through the press. They did relate to council-stock housing and rehousing was certainly an element in some cases. Of course in this case the reporter is an employed tenant with the power to move elsewhere, and this helps to buck any sort of trend. Furthermore, Penhill represents only around a quarter of the housing built for council stock in the town, yet very few reports come from the other areas.

In our research the name Penhill has also been linked with ghost-hunters. Swindon has seen a fair few short-lived ghost-hunting groups over the years. Newspaper articles from the 1960s to the present decade show that almost all the featured ghost hunters live or lived in the Penhill estate.

Why does Penhill, of all the residential areas in the town, have such a link with experiencing and investigating paranormal phenomena? It is almost impossible to say, but everyone is free to draw their own conclusions.

The new housing estate of Abbey Meads is the setting for an alleged haunting of a family home in Colman Park. Ethically the name of the family and the exact location of the house cannot be provided, but the family comprises a father, 36, mother, 27, and two daughters aged five and two at the time of writing.

The Abbey Meads estate is a modern development of private homes, the first stage of the Northern Expansion of Swindon. Development started in 1993 with 800 houses and the full 2,700 houses were constructed over the following seven years. Part of the estate's land was purchased from the Hitchin family in 1982, and was known as Abbey Farm. The estate itself is part of the parish of Blunsdon St Andrew. The nearby village of Blunsdon dates back to the Iron Age, although, at the time of the publication of the Domesday Book in 1086, its population comprised just three adult males.

The Abbey Meads estate (named after the ruined Blunsdon Abbey in the village) was known to be farmland and fields at least from the 17th century onwards. The area known as Groundwell Ridge, just to the north of the site, was found to contain Roman remains in 1996. The archeological site was described by English Heritage as 'one of the most important Roman finds in England'; there is evidence of a possible Roman bath and village site, with artefacts dating back to AD100.

There is currently a debate within the field of paranormal research as to whether the age of currently standing buildings, or the land they stand on, has some impact on whether haunting cases are prevalent. This argument is based purely on anecdotal evidence and seems to have little bearing in reality. Older buildings are, perhaps, more likely to appear spooky and therefore produce haunting claims and, of course, older buildings have had more chance to produce historical and

Abbey Meads is a new build estate, perhaps Swindon's most modern 'haunting site' in Colman Park.

folkloric claims of ghosts. This has little impact in current and ongoing cases of hauntings, where a house built in the last decade is just as capable of producing a haunting as a house built centuries ago. This is certainly the case in this modern family home in Colman Park.

All four members of the family, who have lived in the house since 2005, claim to have been affected. The father described his experience to us on behalf of the family. 'Both me and my wife have heard a girl calling for "mum". We have both answered "yes", thinking it was our eldest daughter upstairs, but she said she never said anything at the time. What really got us spooked was when our daughter was in the conservatory but both me and my wife heard a voice from upstairs.' He continued:

'My wife has been touched on her head twice, once on the stairs and once in a computer room/bedroom. The very latest occurrence is the sound of footsteps which myself and [my] daughters have heard. The first time was when my wife was putting our youngest daughter to bed, while my oldest was in our bed. Our eldest came into the bedroom my wife was in and said she didn't want to be alone in our bedroom as she could hear footsteps. My wife said they were probably from outside but my daughter said she could hear them walking around the bed. The next time was when both our daughters were playing in the conservatory, when they both ran out with my eldest saying she could hear footsteps in there and neither of them would go back in there that day. The last time was when I heard what I thought was my wife walking up the stairs while I was in our en suite, when I came out she was downstairs so I asked if she had just been upstairs but she said she hadn't.'

Haunting cases seem often to spring from a certain event. One unexplained event can lead a family to the conclusion that they have a haunting. It would be inappropriate to try to draw conclusions about whether this first encounter was paranormal or otherwise. Was this voice calling for 'mum' really inexplicable? Or was it a person outside, or at a nearby house, or a noise coming from a TV or radio? Without firm evidence, PSI cannot say for certain. Unfortunately, once a home is labelled as haunted, it is likely that natural noises and feelings can then been seen in light of the haunting claim, and can seem to back it up. Whether these occurrences were the result of this expectation, or genuinely unexplained phenomena, it is impossible to say. At the time of writing, the presumed haunting has decreased somewhat, so it is possible PSI may never know what happened at Colman Park.

A 200-year-old cottage, subsumed by the sprawling urbanisation of Swindon, was the setting for a decade-long haunting reported by the Tully family, formerly of Hyde Road. Hyde Road is part of the council-designated Urban Conservation Area of Kingsdown, Stratton St Margaret. The area of special architectural and historical interest has been earmarked for preservation. It intersects with the Arkells Brewery, built in 1861 just north of what was then the village of Stratton St Margaret. By the turn of the century, a hamlet known as Kingsdown had grown around the brewery, comprising a few houses and cottages set in open land. The former Tully residence was thought to be a 200-year-old cottage in this hamlet. Stratton was known as Stratone in the Domesday Book of 1086, named for the Latin word for street – 'strata' – after the Roman road running through the area. As Swindon expanded through the 20th century, the villages and hamlets were swallowed by the urban mass and are now not distinguishable as individual settlements.

Over the course of 10 years, various apparently paranormal incidents were witnessed by the Tully family and their friends. These included an instance of being near to the chest of drawers in the bedroom and hearing a thud, and finding the whole contents of the sock drawer to have been thrown to the floor. Also, the family would find that kitchen forks had been, bizarrely, placed under floor rugs with no hint as to how they got there. Another time, the lady of the house was walking around in her dressing gown, as she sometimes would, and suddenly felt the sensation of the cord being tugged despite no one being anywhere near her. Similarly, a family guest felt the back of their jumper being pulled and stretched. The strangest aspect of this episode is that the lady of the house

actually witnessed the jumper being pulled and stretched. On various other occasions over the years, the front door opened, seemingly of its own accord, and a friend visiting the house once saw this.

The former lady of the house described to us her encounters with a spiritualist medium that came to the house:

'Finally when things kept occurring I requested, through a friend of a friend, a spiritualist to come round (free of charge, I will add!) and seek solace for the "troubled spirits".

'While releasing the spirits another friend of mine, who wanted to witness this occasion, saw a large shopping bag's handle rise up in the air and twist around another person's legs. I was not there at the time because I didn't want to be part of it, the incidents troubled me enough!'

Hyde Road in Stratton.

The area pre-dates the expanding urban Swindon which subsumed it.

'The night after the spiritualist left and I returned home, my husband and I were talking about all what had happened and I said: "Still, all seven of the spirits have been released from their state of transition", and 'lo and behold the bike that was leaning against the wall fell from the wall and it had been propped there for hours before! Coincidences or not, I don't know!'

The Hyde Road case is perhaps one of the more compelling haunted house reports. Often hauntings appear only to happen to one or two individuals, sometimes suggesting it is more to do with their attitudes and beliefs than anyone else, but events in Hyde Road took place over a long period with several independent witnesses. Another tell-tale sign is where a person seems to experience hauntings in numerous locations – again, is it more to do with the person than the environment? – but the family's experiences seem to be confined to this property. Furthermore, occasional events, such as the stretching of the jumper, were experienced by more than one person. While many of these paranormal experiences are explainable by natural means, they are not all explicable without further investigation.

One thing that is striking about this case is the absence of a ghost – a figure seen or some apparent communication attempted – with the exception of a spiritualist medium identifying spirits after the event. The compelling idea remains that some aspects of hauntings are in the perceptions of the individual – after all, why would a ghost be to blame for a series of strange events? – but the specific details of the Hyde Road haunting make the case of great interest.

CASE: TYDEMAN STREET, GORSE HILL   TYPE: RECENT

A man who used to live in Tydeman Street in the Gorse Hill area of Swindon got in touch to tell us about his experiences at his family home there. Gorse Hill itself is an area of Victorian-built red-brick terraces constructed in around the 1890s as part of the expansion of New Swindon to accommodate the railway industry. These are the man's experiences, in his own words:

'It all started in the early 1990s when I was very sceptical of the paranormal but was cajoled into visiting a renowned fortune-teller in the area. She was uncannily accurate in my past, and the then present, and events that have happened to date she also predicted. However, she also startled me by telling me that I was far more psychic than she was but that I needed to open my mind.

'Since then I have had many unexplained events occurring: a baby walker playing its musical tune in the middle of night (only plays when it is moved) and going downstairs to find it exactly in the same place as it was left. My wife discovered the buckle on her satchel bag had been mysteriously reversed, meaning she was unable to close the bag.

'Electrical items have not worked correctly, for example televisions turning themselves off, even though we were nowhere near the controls. Then when we turned it [the television] back on it almost immediately switched off again. This happened on numerous occasions. One time our video recorder reset its timing date to 1985 and then the same thing happened to our in-laws video recorder while I was there.

'Unexplained loud noises and crashes were heard that were over and above the normal household noises. One in particular was in the middle of a still summer night and was akin to someone picking up the draining board full of crockery and throwing it to the floor. But on checking immediately there was nothing there.

'My daughter, who was only three at the time, suddenly asked if a man with a black hat used to live in this house – we put it down to her imagination – but then discovered that indeed in the

Tydeman Street in Gorse Hill.

The site of a recent alleged haunting.

1920s a man with a black hat lived in the house. We were put in contact with his daughter, who used to live in our house, and she believed it to be her father who always wore a black hat when delivering papers and cigarettes.'

This seems to be a case of an individual man who had never experienced paranormal phenomena in his life, who, following a convincing fortune-telling and being told he was psychic, began to experience a great deal of haunting phenomena. The spiritualist answer as to why this happened may be that his eyes were opened to psychic events by the fortune-teller, and he then began to experience everything around him that he had previously ignored. The rationalist explanation may consider that hauntings were not part of his consciousness before he was cajoled – his own words – into seeing a fortune-teller. Our perceptions of the world can be drastically altered by a single profound event, such as the apparently accurate prediction of a series of events. This can even inspire belief in the paranormal where none existed previously. An individual being told, by what is now a figure of authority, that they are psychic can create a strong sense of expectation. In the mind of a person who believes in and expects paranormal events, odd things that would previously have gone unnoticed suddenly become very important.

It is not ethical for us to judge the experiences that happened to this man on Tydeman Street, but everyone is free to make up their own minds.

CASE: PRIVATE HOMES IN SOUTH MARSTON   TYPE: HISTORIC, ONGOING

South Marston is a small village four miles north-east of Swindon. The name Marston presumably derives from the common English village name meaning marsh farm. The village is said to date from the pre-Domesday Saxon period. It is not mentioned by name in the Domesday Book of 1086 although local commentators have suggested that there is evidence that the area was owned personally by William I, and was therefore exempt from registration in the book.

The Roman remains discovered around the village suggest early occupation, supported by the proximity to the Ermin Street Roman road. By the Victorian period there were fewer than 500 inhabitants, mainly agricultural workers, and this declined further in the 20th century as workers moved into Swindon. Since World War Two the village has expanded and looks set to increase further by allowing the building of new housing on brownfield sites.

South Marston seems to have its fair share of folkloric ghost tales, but the mid-1990s saw the local newspaper – stimulated by the visit of unnamed 'ghost busters' – report two simultaneous poltergeist cases in the small village. One house's inhabitants claim to have heard footsteps from their upstairs floor and so-called haunted carol singing – what this is, is not made clear! – in the 19th-century house. They also asserted that their dog barked at thin air, that doors opened and closed of their own accord and that bedclothes appeared to be pulled back in unused bedrooms. The occupants decided to make an historical attribution and blamed their ghost activity on one of the elderly Clarke sisters, who lived at the house some 100 years before.

A nearby farmhouse claimed to have experienced poltergeist activity for no fewer than 30 years. One occupant told the *Evening Advertiser*: 'First a plate flew off the wall in the dining room. Then a mirror leapt off the wall, hit me on the hand and shattered into a thousand pieces.' The family claimed a workman 'fled in terror' as he worked alone in their house and heard voices. However, their children felt unnerved by odd noises. The adults also reported moving furniture and 'flying forks'. After trying prayers to remove the spirit, the family called on an Anglican priest, who promptly performed an exorcism. However, the family reported a return by the poltergeist after a two-week holiday.

Apparently the National Museum of Photography, Film and Television installed round-the-clock surveillance cameras to try to capture the ghost, with the hope of presenting it at Britain's first X-Files exhibition later that year.

These ghost tales seem to be a part of a sharp upturn in haunting accounts from the mid-1990s to date. As the X-Files exhibition aspect of the story suggests, this renaissance might be somewhat media driven. It is clear that the media inspires researchers of paranormal activity and, therefore, unspoken tales of many years, like that of the farmhouse, suddenly come to light. However, the extent to which the media drives experiencers of haunted houses to have these experiences in the first place is less clear.

South Marston village saw more than one case in the mid-1990s.

Blunsdon is a large village approximately one mile north of the urban mass of Swindon. There is evidence of Roman occupation of the site of the village and the A419 dual carriageway, which intersects the village, lies on the course of the Ermin Street Roman road that linked Cirencester to Silchester. The road this private home lays on was the ancient by-way that intersected with Ermin Street. The house itself is a modern build in a semi-isolated position, away from the main road. The current resident has described her experiences:

'On many occasions when sitting on the sofa in the front room I have seen a flash of light from outside of the house, coming from the same corner, almost like the flash of a camera when a photo is taken. Enough to make me turn my head and look. This usually happens when I am at home on my own. On several occasions I've also felt as if someone is standing in the doorway to the front room; again when I'm on my own, enough to make me turn around and even go out into the corridor to see if anyone is there.

'A few weeks ago when I bought a new hat I hung it on the hat stand in the corridor and on three occasions I had found the hat lying on the floor next to the door of the spare bedroom. This would usually be when I'd gone out; I'd come back and find the hat on the floor. I'd tried knocking the hat stand and there was no way you could have knocked it off. It was a good four feet from the hat stand, too far away if it had been the case that it had fallen off.

'I've quite often felt as if there is someone else in the house, heard noises as if to suggest there is someone else here. I've looked around convinced there was someone else here, like the landlord, who has a key, but there has been no one around. I've also felt a strong sense of

presence in the grounds of the house, at night, when I've been walking down the track on my own. Or if I had been going up on my own to go next door. My partner has also felt an unusual feeling and seen odd shadows when walking through the grounds.

'One particular night stands out in my mind. On that night my partner had woken me up to tell me there was someone coming in the front door. He had not been to sleep yet and was sitting up in bed, reading. He said it was clearly the sound of someone opening the outside door, which is opposite our bedroom door. As we were making to get out of bed to find out what was going on something else happened. My partner heard and saw the handle to our bedroom door going down sharply as if someone was opening it from the other side and he called out to find out who was there and at

The hat was found several feet from the hanging place.

The door handle, which unaccountably turned.

that point it stopped. As I was getting out of bed I did not see the handle but I heard it clearly. We cautiously left the bedroom thinking there was an intruder there. Not only was there no one there but there was a full bin bag propped up against the front door – ready to take out in the morning – which would have prevented anyone from actually opening the outside door.'

The Blunsdon case is a fairly typical example of a haunting without a ghost (that is to say, an apparition) involved. Numerous experiences are highlighted as being unusual and, without a normal explanation to hand, a paranormal conclusion is leapt to. It is perfectly possible that natural explanations could be found for this series of unusual events. For example, psychological factors could be at play in a semi-isolated rural environment to which the residents are not fully accustomed. This is especially the case in the semi-darkness of night, with an orchard nearby whose trees could create shadows. Similarly the flashes of light could have a normal explanation not currently identified. The night-time experience remains interesting. However, any reports made from bed should be treated with caution, as it is perfectly normal for people to temporarily fall asleep without realising.

Historically, the village of Haydon Wick fell into the ancient parochial parish of Rodbourne Cheney and was administered by the civil council of Highworth. The 1841 census shows fewer than 400 residents, a number not greatly changed in the census of 1961. Prior to this time, the village mainly comprised the Victorian-build houses of Blunsdon Road and High Street, along with a number of farms. These streets are now, according to the census of 2001, at the heart of a residential Haydon Wick of some 11,000 people, and entirely subsumed by the growing town of Swindon.

On the old high street is the Fox and Hounds pub. Like much of the street, the pub is an older building, set in the modern urban area. One of the pub residents discussed her experiences of the flat upstairs:

'I've been a local in the pub for 15 to 20 years and never experienced anything strange. I'm quite a sceptic and the idea of ghosts had never even occurred to me.

'When I moved into the flat above the pub, about six years ago, the occasional strange thing started to happen. At this time people also began to say to me they thought there was a ghost in the pub. Nothing much ever happened downstairs in the pub, except for the occasional glass smashed to the floor where it had been firmly place on the shelf.

The Fox and Hounds at Haydon Wick.

'However, a year or so after I moved into the flat something strange did happen. A friend came to visit and brought her little girl. It was just me in the flat and we were moving around together. We went to the bedroom to get the washing, which took us past the front room.

'My friend asked me if that was my front room and I said it was. She then asked "who was that stood by your window?" I asked what she meant. She said there had been someone there but was not there now. There was not anyone in the flat.

'On talking to my father about this he had said that when he was a boy and used to come here he would often see unusual things in that upstairs room.

'When I got a new Jack Russell dog it started to behave strangely in that room. For about three weeks it would do little else but sit by that exact same window just growling.

'My flatmate that now lives in the flat with me has never actually seen anything. Neither have I and nor do I particularly want to!'

The Paranormal Site Investigators team hopes to pay a visit to the Fox and Hounds to look into the validity of this case.

CASE: HIGH STREET, HAYDON WICK   TYPE: RECENT, ONGOING

The other case in Haydon Wick is also based on the old High Street. One tenant of a Victorian building on High Street was told about a resident ghost as he was about to move into the house:

'We have lived here in Haydon Wick for two years and the chap we bought the house from, when we picked up the keys, told us about the "ghost". He said she was called Edith. We have a lot of records from the past of the house, going back to 1850, but we cannot find any record of an Edith. The house dates back to this time when it was a Cider House, there was a row of cottages where our garden currently is. The man who sold us our house said that Edith is an older lady, and very friendly: they had never had any issues with her. They told us they heard her moving around sometimes and felt her presence. He didn't tell us about Edith until the sale had gone through, although it didn't bother us as we'd lived and worked in haunted places in the past.

'The house was extended back in the 1970s. The "ghost" only seems to be in the older part of the house. We could hear her in the upstairs walking on the floor boards; a definite sound of footsteps and creaking floorboards. We have a toddler who, at the time, was about 9 months old; when she was sitting in the high chair she would smile and point and wave to something behind you. But as always when you turned around there would be absolutely nothing there. Also the cat would act oddly at certain times. But we would just say, "oh Edith's about again!"

'At the beginning of 2007, I think it was, there was a week-long period when, after we had gone to bed, the hot tap (and only the hot one for some reason) kept turning itself on full pelt. I know that there is nothing wrong with the plumbing as we had had a new bathroom fitted. I had a word with one of the girls at work who is into all this stuff and she told us to ask her to stop, and that we didn't mind her being here. So we did this and sure enough it stopped.

'Sadly our house was flooded during last summer and the house has been totally stripped out. However, since then we have not had any contact from her at all.

'When we took the old ceiling down we found a wedding ring. We don't know if this is lost, or who it belonged to, but we do intend to replace it.'

The Haydon Wick case certainly has the typical signs of the modern haunt: the feeling of presence, creaking floorboards and taps behaving oddly following a refit. Where someone experiences such things in another place, they might not conclude they have a ghost: such experiences might be relatively common and normal in older

The old High Street.

The Haydon Wick High Street existed as part of the separate village.

houses. It was perhaps inevitable that the events had been looked for and interpreted as a haunting as the occupants were told of a ghost and had experienced ghost activity earlier in their lives. It is not possible to draw firm conclusions about the nature of haunting experiences unless you are there. Whether the Haydon Wick case was a simple case of misattribution or something more is impossible to say with any certainty.

CASE: FORMER ARMY BASE BUNGALOWS, STANTON FITZWARREN

TYPE: BLACK DOG APPARITION

Apparitions of black dogs are a peculiarly British folkloric category. There have been dozens of reported sightings from all over the British Isles over many years.

In the various writings on the subject, Swindon and Wiltshire do not seem to have a following of the black dog trend. However, the Secretary of the Highworth Historical Society has heard folkloric rumours of a black dog story in Inglesham, a small village just on the other side of Highworth from Stanton Fitzwarren. The Inglesham dog is said to stalk the former railway line. There are also legends of the black dog of Toothill and a black dog that was, in times before total urbanisation, said to walk the road from Moredon to Haydon Wick.

The interpretation of black dogs varies from region to region: in many places the appearance of such beasts is said to be an omen of death. Black dogs are also considered to be the guardians of the underworld in European folklore.

Tales of black dogs are often associated with specific geographic locations and appear to have progressed from local folklore. In some areas black dogs are said to be stories made up by parents to warn children from entering certain areas, such as graveyards, and as a method of passing on societal norms such as respecting places where the dead rest. It has often been suggested that knowledge of such folkloric traditions has led to hallucination, although there are numerous accounts of groups of people seeing such apparitions. Another explanation advanced has been the simple misperception of a normal animal. None of these explanations seem to apply to an experience reported by Barbara Ann Humphries now living in Highworth, a small town just outside Swindon:

'My experience was during the 1940s, when I was a little girl of five or six years old. We were evacuated during World War Two. At one time we were located in the Ministry of Defence (MOD) bungalows attached to the former army base in Stanton Fitzwarren.

Stanton Fitzwarren village is the site of Swindon's best documented 'black dog' case.

'One night I was sleeping in bed. We were scared of the dark so we had a pouffe that would prop open the door of our bedroom to let the light in from the hallway. That night I woke up and looked over and saw a big black dog that looked like an Alsatian. It was sitting on the pouffe and its eyes were glowing orange in the moonlight. I turned over and looked at the wall because I was so scared.

'Later my father came in and I refused to get out of bed, telling him there was a big dog there. He told me to stop being so silly, and that there had never been a dog in the house.

'On the Monday morning the school coach arrived at the bungalows to pick me up and I told all the other kids about the big dog I saw in the bedroom. They all piped up and told me I had seen the "ghost dog of Stanton".'

Apparently the children recalled a tale of a ghost dog that belonged to a soldier who was billeted to the camp. The dog was said to wander the roads of the village and the nearby woods, looking for its soldier master. This black dog tale described by the school children seems consistent with most folklore black dog warning stories. As mentioned earlier, this sort of warning could have developed to stop children venturing onto the roads at night, and similarly to get them to stay away from the local woods. Presumably the existing ghost story of Stanton Woods, as described in the Stanton Farmhouse chapter, was not enough to keep the children away!

It is worth noting that the girl of this story seemed to be surprised about the black dog story and, not being from the area, it is possible she did not know of it before her experience. While her knowing and forgetting about it is possible, it seems unlikely that the expectation following a scary story could have led to a misperception.

Black dog researcher Dr Simon Sherwood, of the University of Northampton, does note on his website that, in rare cases, black dog apparitions are seen shortly after sleep and that hypnopompic imagery could be at play. In this state, between sleeping and waking, psychologists have established that very vivid visual, tactile and auditory hallucinations are possible.

The Borough of Swindon has few well-documented haunting cases but the King and Queen pub in Highworth is one of the exceptions. The 500-year-old pub, in the High Street of the ancient outlying town, has reported half a dozen cases since the late 1960s. Unconfirmed historical reports claim the building was once part of an old monastery. It is perhaps fitting, then, that the first identified sighting was of the monk that is said to haunt various places in the town. He is said to resemble a hunch-backed

Highworth's King & Queen has reported many stories over the decades – the High Street represents a 'cluster' of cases.

figure in white robes. Local legend tells that the monk broke his chastity vows and was tried in the building and hanged in the alleyway outside.

In 1968 the sound of a whining dog was said to wake the then landlord. The landlord reported seeing a motionless figure of a monk. When the dog was set free to attack the presumed intruder it apparently froze in fear. The landlord reported approaching the figure himself, which then glided straight through a wall. Reports from this era also include footsteps being heard, on various occasions, from the area of the pub said to be an old courtroom. Upon investigation there was never anyone in the vicinity.

At around the same time a visiting engineer was enjoying a quiet drink and happened to mention to the landlord of the time the loud footsteps he heard from above, and was surprised to find out there was no one up there.

The story of the monk re-emerged several times in the 21st century, when the pub came under new management. On Hallowe'en 2000 a columnist from the local newspaper was invited to tour the supposedly haunted bar. While the journalist claimed to feel nothing, he did recount a local story of a spot in the bar that dogs are said to bark at for no apparent reason.

The following Hallowe'en the new pub owners claimed their scepticism about paranormal events was fading. One staff member recounted his experiences to the local newspaper, the then *Evening Advertiser*:

'Sometimes it is very warm here and the temperature can suddenly drop and you get a cold shudder. There have been flickering lights and sometimes, when you turn all the switches off at night, you come down in the morning and a light has come back on.

'Some of the regulars have been talking about a chap who went to use the toilets outside and came back as white as a sheet. He couldn't tell them what happened but afterwards said he had seen an apparition.

'When I was here for the first year I didn't believe a thing but would still be worried sometimes at night. It is a very old pub so there are cracks, bangs and groans anyway, but when you see shadows out of the corner of your eye, you start to think.'

The newspaper reports that the pub has become quite a tourist attraction, with guests staying in the pub overnight hoping to witness the spectral monk for themselves. In early 2003 the pub updated the *Evening Advertiser* with more recent accounts of the alleged haunting:

'On occasion I have switched off all the lights before going to bed but on coming down the next morning a corner of the pub is lit. And just a few years ago when we still let out bedrooms a guest woke up one morning covered in thin scratches. Sometimes people who had booked in for a few weeks would come down after a couple of days and check out.

'There have even been guests who said they heard footsteps coming from the attic, which runs above the bedrooms. But no one ever goes up there. It hasn't been touched for 150 years and still contains horse hair and hay from when it was used as stables.

'I haven't seen the ghost but there have been some strange things happening which I've witnessed. The most recent occurred while I was chatting to a customer at the bar and suddenly two pint glasses smashed. They just seemed to explode. It wasn't as if they had just come out of the dishwasher and cracked. It was weird. No one was hurt and I don't think the ghost is out to get anybody. And about a month ago my dad ... was cashing-up one night and saw what he thought was [a member of staff]. But when he came down from the office he was told [he] wasn't even in the pub.

'The office upstairs is freezing even if we put the heating on. It never warms up.

'Most people are sceptical though and don't think much of it – but it makes you wonder.'

The King and Queen in Highworth, is one of few cases in Swindon that can provide a direct comparison between the accounts of today and 30 years earlier. There is a theory that the popular media can drive the ghost accounts. Many sightings start with ambiguous events that people blame on the ghost and this case seems to provide some anecdotal evidence of this. A predominant theme of ghost stories in decades past was seeing a figure that disappeared. The television trend in the early years of the 20th century included cold spots and scratching of individuals. The trend also seemed popular in the rest of the town, where apparition sightings were common from the 1930s and similarly, electronic interference, cold spots and noises are the norm today.

CASE: HIGHWORTH TUNNELS TYPE: HISTORICAL, LEGEND

Every town has its legends of tunnels, usually running for miles beneath the old quarter of the town. Such networks are almost always said to connect the churches, old manor houses, local pubs and old makeshift courthouses (also pubs). Very few towns can provide much evidence for these folkloric rumours, with the exception of the occasional pub and building with a larger than average cellar that claims to be one brick wall away from the much-heralded network.

Swindon is no exception to the tunnels rule. Tunnels are said to stretch across Old Town, linking pubs and houses to the old manor house. There seems to be little evidence to back up these claims, beyond the large cellar discovered at the famous Villet's House, which is being developed into flats.

Highworth, too, passes on legends of tunnels connecting the church, pubs and various local buildings, but it also has a genuine set of tunnels. The tunnels lie buried beneath the garden of a local historian at her home on Cricklade Road, just off High Street. They do not claim to be a town-wide network but were originally connected to nearby Westrop House and ran down to the family's stables. They were used by their servants for storing beehives and contained an ice-house where ice would last for up to three years. The water to form it was collected from Sevenhampton

Lake. However, bees and ice are apparently not the only inhabitants of these tunnels. One night a man witnessed a white female figure waft out of the tunnel entrance. So frightened was he by what he had seen, that he never returned there again. There are also reports that she has knocked on the door of neighbouring Westrop House. The historian has recounted her knowledge of the rumours:

'A chap used to keep is motorbike down in the tunnels and he came home one night at gone midnight and he saw this white shape coming out of the mouth of the tunnel. It frightened him so much he changed where he kept his motorbike. It was supposed to be the lady friend of William Crowdy who had the house built.

One of the tunnel entrances.

There is little doubt of the 'spooky' context of the tunnels .

The tunnels are perhaps the largest open network in the borough.

He used, apparently, to meet her in the summerhouse and his wife knew nothing about it. You can believe that if you will. I don't! I think it was too much port after dinner, usually, and bad lighting.'

William Crowdy is the subject of much local folklore. He is said to have been a solicitor and has been seen wandering around the streets of the town with a rope wrapped around his neck. The connection of the William Crowdy legend to the tunnels is another classic example of attaching an unusual experience to someone who famously died at a location, thus transforming an odd experience into a ghostly legend.

Although recognised as the only 13th-century church in the borough, Christian worship has occurred on the site of St Michael's, Highworth, at least as far back as 1086. Despite such a lengthy history, it is only since the early 20th century that the church has been associated with the spectre of a monk.

During a late afternoon in 1910 two men, stood by the south door, were surprised to be passed by a stooped, hunchbacked figure in a white robe. More curious, if not horrifying, was the apparition's face: grey and featureless with the exception of dark shadows where eyes should have been. During a November evening some 26 years later, the verger of St Michael's encountered a seemingly identical form. On this occasion it was observed silently walking the central aisle inside the church, passing through a closed curtain towards the west door. The three most recently documented sightings of this figure all occurred in 1970; at the altar, in the churchyard and walking the short roadway between St Michael's and the ruins of Highworth's monastery.

Popular opinion considers this apparition to be one and the same as the monk historically seen at the King and Queen inn on High Street. Circumstantial evidence supporting a link between the pair exists within rumours of an underground passageway joining the two locations with the old monastery. If these associations are correct and correspond with local folk-tales, the apparition is that of a monk cruelly executed for breaching his vows of celibacy. Some may consider that his appearances at St Michael's Church represent little more than an extension of the area his wretched spirit now wanders.

Yet while folk-tales considered in isolation can deliver a compelling argument for the existence of ghost, a wider study of myth and legend can present a counterbalance. Stories of spectral monks are synonymous with the areas adjacent to demolished monasteries. This may initially seem

The church is adjacent to the High Street 'cluster'.

Reports were documented until the 1970s.

reasonable enough, as one would expect to find the ghost of a cleric at a religious site. However, many apparitions take a classic, if not archetypal form; examples are the monk, coach and horses, highwayman, Cavalier and grey lady. By comparison, apparitions of undistinguished, plain and non-uniformed individuals are disproportionately few. Three speculative explanations are worth exploring and relate directly to the ghost of St Michael's Church.

Firstly, many of these archetypal ghosts are associated with specific locations, particularly those in reasonably sheltered or isolated places where well-intentioned visitors would be few and far between. Children, vandals and thieves may have all been deterred from exercising mischief in light of a possible encounter with the supernatural.

Secondly, those of a sceptical nature may argue that witnesses at St Michael's Church have seen, hallucinated or imagined something unusual but not paranormal. By seizing upon both the ambience of their surroundings and prior knowledge of local folklore, these witnesses have misattributed what they observed to be a monk.

Finally, there is the possibility that at least one witness report was a hoax, and a monk would surely represent a likely subject to associate with a church. There is anecdotal evidence to support this possibility; the two men who claimed to have seen the monk in 1910 were not alone at the south door at the time of their sighting. A woman, arranging church flowers, was also present but proved unable to substantiate the tale presented by the pair. Subsequent sightings may have been the result of misattribution by witnesses primed by their knowledge of the ghost story.

In the absence of any solid evidence to support one particular theory over another, events at St Michael's Church should be considered with due caution and balance. If nothing else, one should ask why such a historic ghost has appeared only in very recent times.

In any area, ghost stories go in and out of fashion over time. Highworth in the late 1960s seemed to be teeming with tales of apparitions wandering the small town. As reported elsewhere, the figure of a monk was seen at the King and Queen on High Street in 1968. This event seemed to excite much conversation, even, apparently, leading to tourists visiting the town over the following months.

Pentylands Lane exists more or less in the same state as when reports were made in the 1960s.

Stories surfacing in the middle of 1969 included a haunted house in Church Street. The local newspaper, then the *Evening Advertiser*, spoke to a woman who had lived there some years earlier who claimed 'Nellie would never sleep in the back bedroom, as she said she had seen a monk there, so her mother stayed in the room with her one night and they heard someone coming into the room. They both fled, and they always kept the bedroom boarded up after that.'

It was reported that the monk would rise from the floorboards, apparently from a tunnel underneath that led to St Michael's Church. Also recalled was a house at the end of High Street that contained a table that seemingly rose by itself, while candles would extinguish themselves. The series of events led the local paper to assert that 'Highworth has suddenly become a ghost town.' Meanwhile, locals remembered the tales of deceased local solicitor William Crowdy wandering the streets of the town.

Perhaps inevitably, this very public fixation with ghost stories took hold of the imagination of local young people. In nearby Swindon 'ghostbusting' schoolchildren from Old Town's Commonweal School were investigating various cases of hauntings, including houses in Penhill, Deacon Street and Hinton Manor. Not to be outdone, the young people of Highworth set off searching for ghosts in the semi-rural Pentylands Lane. Apparently an apparition presented itself to no fewer than 20 children. One boy told the local newspaper:

'It was about 10.30pm and there was a full moon. We saw this thing lying flat out on the top of the tractor. Then it got up. It looked disfigured, deformed; it was a kind of shining white. It could have been a boy or a small child, about 4ft 6in tall. It seemed to stand by the tractor and then it started moving towards us. We were scared. It seemed to know what we were doing. We walked up the lane and it followed us along the hedge. Then it followed us back again. We got out quick.'

Two further episodes, an hour apart, followed the next night. A group of seven young people, including the brother of the boy who made the first report, saw a 'bent, white figure' floating several feet from the ground and heading for the hedge. The second group reported a similar experience.

In the days and weeks following, a 4ft grey shape was seen on the verge, and a legless mist with an outstretched hand pointed towards another group and then sat on a gate. Another girl reported that the ghost 'touched her on the head' while riding her horse, and the horse refused to continue moving.

While these stories abounded, rumours went round of previous deaths on Pentylands Lane, including a man drowning in a pond, another being killed by a tractor and a further man dying following being kicked by a horse.

It seems a distinct possibility that the adult population of the town discussing monks, solicitors and paranormal goings-on wandering the streets of the town had inspired their childrens' imaginations. Mass hysteria is perhaps the most compelling cause for 20 children claiming to see a hunchbacked ghost, with similar reports by various related groups in the days and weeks that followed. After reaching a crescendo in late 1969 the whole town of Highworth seemed to stop talking about ghosts for the 1970s – presumably it went out of fashion again!

Lydiard House is one of only two widely-recognised folklore hauntings in the borough. Such folklore hauntings are the 'classic' hauntings. These ghost stories usually centre on famous historical figures whose lives were touched by tragedy and whose spirits are destined to roam their ancestral homes. Most gazetteers of hauntings only report Lydiard and the Clifton in their accounts of Swindon. Lydiard is actually set in a village that now borders on the sprawling urban mass of the town. The house itself is a 15th-century Palladian house, one of Wiltshire's smaller stately homes, set in a 260-acre country park that is now maintained by Swindon Borough Council.

Before the Swindon Corporation purchased the estate in 1943, the then abandoned house had belonged to the St John family for over five centuries. Portraits of the family now hang in the museum that the house is home to. The house itself has maintained many original features and includes a room dedicated to the 18th-century resident and society artist Lady Diana Spencer. The park, which has been open to the public daily since 1955, also boasts the restored lawns, lake and arboretum.

The historical haunting centres on Sir John St John, a 17th-century owner who was created a baronet in 1611 and is said to have died in his sixties of natural causes. Sir John's tragedy, said to tie him to the property, was losing his three sons in the king's service during the English Civil War. The victorious Parliamentarians drove the Royalist Sir John to destitution.

Sir John's life certainly fulfils the tragic element that such folkloric legends rely upon. The other characteristics of such hauntings tend to include an element of replay backed up by anecdotal modern experiences. These replays often involve the tragic figure wandering their former domain, apparently unaware of their surroundings. The Lydiard tale follows this folklore, with the tale of an elderly gentleman, assumed to be Sir John, seen gently traversing the grounds at all times of day.

Lydiard House, which is adjacent to the West Swindon area.

The park is popular with visitors, but it has produced its fair share of stories.

Lydiard is Swindon's answer to a stately home.

One modern day anecdote of Sir John's apparition, reported on the website of a Wiltshire newspaper group, deviates from tradition in the apparition's apparent interaction with a group of pensioners who were picnicking in the grounds. The modern legend claims that one pensioner was unable to find a seat and was guided to a vacant chair by a kindly and courteous gentleman. It is unknown why the pensioner attributed the encounter to the apparition of St John. In recent years the folkloric tradition of superstition has been followed. The newspaper group site reports the comments of the house warden in 1989: 'You can always tell when he's around. The temperature drops dramatically, I get goosepimples and sometimes he has a distinctive sweet and sickly smell. It could be the smell of decay I suppose – he has been dead since 1648.'

Such superstitious attributions are not uncommon. The spirit is often seen as a friendly and reassuring figure that, in this case, is blamed for unusual environmental fluctuations. The current curator of the house recounts the tradition of a room that is always cold. While she has experienced no sightings herself, the legend is kept alive by reports of objects moving when no one is near to them.

More Swindon Hauntings: Pubs, Rumours and Legends

So far *Haunted Swindon* has largely steered clear of the traditional ghost story or legend in favour of critical analysis of first-hand, modern-day ghost experiences.

Despite the rational emphasis of the book, no picture of a town's haunted heritage would be complete without documenting the haunted pubs, the rumours of hauntings past or present (undocumented oral traditions) and the legends of years gone by. Each classification has its own compelling features, but we start with the seemingly ubiquitous haunted pub.

Haunted Pubs

The adage that every pub has a ghost may be an exaggeration, but only a slight one! If you consider any old rural public house, or any traditional urban 'local', there is a fairly reasonable chance it has had a ghost story attached to it at some stage. Often the tale is etched into the minds of the staff and locals and can be retold verbatim by at least one person who happens to be there at any one time. This certainly applies to rural pubs such as the Jolly Tar, the King and Queen and the urban Clifton, which are expanded upon in other chapters. In other pubs the tradition lies rather low: out of sight or perhaps disappearing all together. The Sun Inn at Coate is a good example. Historical rumours point towards its being haunted but the current staff – and even 'old lags' – have never heard the stories.

So are pubs the most haunted type of building? Scientifically it is difficult to say without a representative survey. From our census of Swindon – which is inevitably incomplete – pubs are certainly the most common type of supposedly haunted building in the borough. Anecdotally they make up a major share of haunted locations exposed in books and TV shows made on the subject. Perhaps the haunted pub is foremost in the consciousness of the public? Certainly when rookie paranormal investigation groups build a caseload of public buildings, the pub is almost always the most prominent feature on their schedule. But why would pubs make the most haunted of buildings? Certainly pubs tend to feature among the oldest buildings in a lot of areas – not that a building has to be old to report a haunting – but the opportunity of centuries for a story to develop certainly helps. Then there is the very public and social nature of the environment. Certainly pubs stand out as buildings with a constant influx of visitors over the course of centuries, long before other buildings were open to the public. The social nature of the pub seems to lead to the telling of stories. Perhaps pubs report more hauntings because the story or tradition is often never lost, in the way that it often is with other buildings? The capacity of a pub to pass on undocumented oral traditions in a pure form is certainly staggering. The current locals of the Jolly Tar will tell of the carpenter who hung the sign of the pub and promptly went home and hanged himself. We were surprised to find the exact same story in an Alfred Williams book of 1912. Nearly a century earlier the same tale was told and, even then, it was not a recent event!

The other consequence of this style of story-telling is that pub hauntings tend to be folkloric and threadbare traditions or, at best, modern misattribution based on the old tales. Here follows some of the more prominent tales of Swindon pub hauntings.

Check Inn (Formerly Black Horse), Wroughton. Type: Modern

This offering from Wroughton was reported in the local newspaper in 1994. An apparent investigating clairvoyant confirmed the pub's haunted status by seeing 'ghostly figures from the upstairs windows of the pub'. She also saw a poem-writing ghost downstairs, which was wearing a 'powdered wig and brocade waistcoat'. The then landlady added: 'In the lounge-bar she said there was a man using a quill pen who was writing a poem and she said it was for us. It was a poem telling us to be happy and not downhearted about anything. Nobody has ever felt frightened in the pub or had bad feelings about it.'

They also remarked that various staff had seen fleeting figures during quiet periods which had, of course, disappeared on closer inspection.

Chiseldon House Hotel. Type: Modern

This modern tale was again reported in the local newspaper in 1995 and, apparently, the story was compelling enough to make it into the *AA's Hotel Guide.*

Reports included pictures being moved, a photocopier turning itself on, telephones being knocked off their hooks, unusual noises and objects being generally flung around.

The then manager was not overly concerned: 'None of us are particularly worried. As far as we are concerned he is one of us. One telephone even moved across the chest of one of our guests while he was lying in bed,' explained Jan. 'We have come to the conclusion that if we have done something he doesn't approve of he will cause disruption.'

Case: Harrow Inn, Wanborough. Type: Folklore

The Harrow reported that, according to local legend, a ghost called old Marlow haunts the building. He was, apparently, a stagecoach driver who crashed outside the inn. He is said to wander the building – at night of course – in 'search of his lost passengers'. The Harrow's website gives an impression of non-concern about this tale that no doubt adds to the pub's charm.

The historical Harrow Inn discusses its 'ghost' on its website.

The 12 Bar (formerly Ship Inn), Town Centre. Type: Folklore
On conversion of the traditional local to a music bar in 2006, the owners told the local newspaper of the rumours: 'One of the things we have been hearing is that the pub is haunted by six ghosts. We haven't seen anything yet, but there are many stories, and we are trying to find out more about the history of the place.'

Nothing might have been experienced, but the claim has certainly caused excitement from some quarters: various paranormalists from around the country have been keen to pay to sit in the pub after closing time.

Former New Inn, Cromwell Street, Town Centre. Type: Historical
This case is something of an oddity, especially as there is no New Inn in Swindon town centre, and no Cromwell Street anywhere in Swindon!

What used to be Cromwell Street and the 1850s pub was demolished in 1970 to make way for the Brunel Shopping Plaza. In a local newspaper article of the same year, the pub's last landlord said: 'I woke up and saw this little kid standing on the pillow. And my wife has got up in the middle of the night because she has heard our children on the landing, but when she looked out of our bedroom there was nothing there.'

The Spotted Cow, Coate. Type: Current
The Spotted Cow has reported various phenomena attributed to a haunting over the last three years. Staff report that activity has seemingly increased over the last 12 months. The haunting reported is not intense, but it is consistent. Reports have included lights flicking on and off of their own accord at night, an eerie feeling of not wanting to be there and the need to run. On one occasion staff were sitting down after closing time and they heard, and discovered, tiles falling off the wall and cutlery smashing onto the floor in the kitchen. In addition, around once every two months, the alarm system is triggered in the middle of the night. The control box records which sensor triggered the alarm. On each occasion a motion sensor —a different one on each occasion — has triggered the alarm rather than being triggered by a door or window being disturbed.

The modern Spotted Cow of Coate image.

The Flag, Town Centre. Type: Current

A 2008 newspaper article claimed that the Flag has experienced hauntings for a number of years, including 'seats moving unexpectedly, keys being moved and strange noises'. Things seemed to come to a head when a friend of the landlady reported capturing an apparent figure on his mobile phone. The landlady told the newspaper:

'It doesn't bother me that much, although the video is quite scary. My friend took it and you can see the black shape in the background. I just want to know what it is and why it's here. I don't see it as a threatening thing. I've had taps on the shoulder and no one's been there. Other people have said they've had their hair pulled. The gas has been turned off before and the music volume goes up and down as if someone's playing with the button.'

One of the landlady's sons added: '[Of the young girl seen in the upstairs hallway] She looked like she was from Victorian times but I could not see her face. It's hard to say how old she is but I've seen her quite a lot. I also saw a man wearing a blazer who quickly stood up at the end of the bar and sat down again before disappearing.'

Unfortunately the footage of the figure is of such low quality that drawing any firm conclusion would be difficult. However, as the figure seems to move with the shaking of the camera, it is possible it is the result of a photographic artefact such as a flare or shadow.

Rumours and threadbare folklore abound about a number of other pubs and bars in Swindon and the surrounding area include the following:

– One paranormal researcher from south Wiltshire is looking into disturbances reported in the Railway Village's Cricketers Arms, Mailcoach and London Street Club.

– The Grove Pub on Drove Road was said by former staff members to be haunted.

– In Old Town the recently closed Goddard Arms was the subject of persistent but non-specific rumours.

– Down the road at the Kings Arms in Wood Street there were rumours of a haunting but the current owners have no knowledge of it.

– In the town centre, bouncers of the former Destiny and Desire and the Brunel nightclubs have claimed to see ghostly figures.

– The Dockle Farmhouse pub in Stratton is said to be haunted by a mischievous ghost of which most of the staff are aware.

– In Toothill, the village tavern is said to be visited by a man in a blue blazer jacket. He has mainly been seen by local kids, but some locals have reported seeing him too.

– Moving in the Highworth direction, there are unconfirmed reports about Jesmonds and another Highworth pub, due to be investigated by the PSI team in 2008, of which no details can be released.

– Finally, staff at the True Heart at Bishopstone have reported seeing strange figures walking around the restaurant.

Rumours of Hauntings Past and Present

The line between rumours, legends and urban myths is often blurred. This section deals with the legends of history, but some overlap is inevitable; these legends include ghostly experiences recited on the Internet, or experiences that people have reported as happening to someone they know, be this a close acquaintance or a 'friend of a friend'. In the rumours will be some truth

– using the word loosely – some misunderstanding, some urban myth retold and possibly stories told to mislead someone, who then passed on the stories as true. As is usually the case with rumours, it is difficult to comment on their evidential status. However, to help build that picture of Swindon's haunted heritage, below is an account of just some of the rumours of haunted Swindon.

On the Mill Lane between Old Town and Wroughton there were rumours of a man who had hanged himself in the 1970s or 1980s. Since then eyewitnesses have reported seeing black figures on the road, and at the nearby manor there have been rumours of anomalous footsteps upstairs and the smell of lavender in one room.

A reliable source in Wroughton told of a strange experience had by someone at a former tennis court in the village. Where the tennis courts used to stand, locals could still, reliably, hear the swish-swish of tennis rackets on occasion. Just south of Wroughton is the mediaeval earthworks known as Barbury Castle. Following reports of ghosts of soldiers – not to mention the odd UFO sighting – the council granted the PSI team access to the site to investigate. Unfortunately nothing of note was uncovered.

According to *Haunted Places of Wiltshire*, Chiseldon villagers have allegedly told of modern experiences of an 'entity of undefined shape' seeming to 'bob along' several feet from the ground and disappear. This tale, taking place in the Church Lane between the village and nearby Hodson, seems curiously similar to the Pentylands Lane account of the 1960s.

Heading east, King Edward's House, near to the village of Wanborough, is said to be haunted by the ghost of a man who hanged himself there. The Edwardian house is currently used as a conference centre.

Northwards, in Hannington, the handsome Hannington Hall is said to have been haunted by monks. Internet forums have discussed a back lane in the village that runs alongside what was once a railway track. The ghostly legend runs that a girl was killed there and presumably is still meant to occasionally appear.

Across in the village of South Marston, there is said to be a presence in the salon within the Nightingale Hotel. On the salon website they offer spiritualist courses and ghost-hunting weekends.

There were reports to the Paranormal Database in 2004–06 of a house on Lambert Close, West Swindon, in which a 'visiting ghost' seemed to throw toys around and manifest over the fire place.

In recent years there have been rumours spread around the Internet by former site staff at the West Swindon Shopping Centre, that the ghost of a man is seen walking the corridors. Similarly, council staff members at the Upper Shaw Farm Community Centre have reported stories of a man who allegedly roams the corridors of the centre at night.

At the community Toothill Farmhouse different eyewitnesses have reported that the figures of two children walk the building.

A woman who lived in Deacon Street in Swindon town in the 1960s was said to have met a deceased old woman standing waiting for her son, who had been killed on a motorbike. Additionally, the girl was said to have died at a Golf Complex and she and her mother are said to be seen from time to time at the top window at one end. Also, staff at a dental surgery in Old Town have reported seeing a little girl wandering around the waiting room after hours when the surgery is shut.

An undisclosed office on Newport Street has reported rumours for years.

An office building in Newport Street has apparently reported regular, ongoing disturbances. Anomalous footsteps and opening of doors were a common feature. The source reported that businesses rarely lasted long in this particular office.

A house at the top of Old Town's Kingshill had residents reporting a man walking through the bedroom wearing a cap and carrying a rucksack. The figure would then climb through the bedroom window and disappear.

One member of staff told us that a whole meeting's worth of people saw a distinct black figure when vacating a mid-morning meeting in the council offices, which formerly housed a school. In addition, two members of staff reported unusual activity in the Spring Gardens multi-storey car park. This included walking through the car park during office hours and being bumped as if knocked into by someone walking fast and too close. On turning round the man found that no one was on the level with him. Another person reported seeing fleeting dark figures on several of the floors. The PSI team did spend an evening investigating the car park – with the consent of the council, of course – but found nothing to report.

Down the road at the Debenhams building there have been persistent rumours over the years of figures being seen in the office corridors above the store.

In nearby Manchester Road one of the shops was said to be haunted in the 1980s. Apparently the ghost of a lady in a long, grey dress was said to walk from the kitchen. Heavy breathing in empty offices was also reported. The nearby Brunel Shopping Centre was said to be haunted by a man who had an accident there in modern times.

North of the railway line, the Greenbridge Retail Park has been the subject of some rumours. Apparently one area of the car park on the McDonald's part of the site has seen spectral nuns walking at night.

Up in Pinehurst, in Poplar Avenue, one man told us that in the 1960s a man was seen walking down the street but was floating a full 6in above the ground. Rumour was later circulated that the man and his mother had committed suicide some years earlier.

Across in Moredon, the former Akers Garage, which has now been demolished, was said to be regularly haunted. Apparently engineers working there would often find that their tools had moved location.

Over in Stratton one of the churches and its churchyard are said, by one witness, to be the scene of ghost replays, in stone tape style, of a nun in a white habit. In the days when Stratton was a separate village, she was known for generally wandering the whole area.

Also in Stratton a school, which will remain nameless as it is still used for that purpose, had rumours of ghosts reported by former students. Another school in Stratton, which has now been demolished, housed a staircase that was out of bounds after a pupil with bad exam results allegedly hanged themselves there. The pupil was alleged to roam the forbidden staircase.

There is also a house, in the Stratton portion of Ermin Street, that estate agents apparently have trouble with to this day. It is said that the house is unsellable due to its haunting and that any previous occupants have been unable to live there for more than a short period of time.

Legends of the Borough of Swindon

Haunting legends span the decades and centuries, often in the form of undocumented oral tradition, or traditions told to authors of local – often self-published, village-based – books and notes. Often these legends are described in earlier decades and centuries and, in some form or another, seem to survive to the present day. Legends from the early 20th century and 19th century often seem to carry warnings that conform to societal norms. These take the form of avoiding certain forms of behaviour, such as pride, greed or curiosity, or simply avoiding dangerous places. Legends often carry the smack of myth or folklore, and there is a certain overlap although, writing in 1885, William Morris notes that such legends were treated seriously, as indisputable fact, even 50 years before he wrote his account of Swindon.

While *Haunted Swindon* is primarily a rationalist book, an appreciation of the history of haunting accounts is important to the understanding of the development and context of how we view ghosts.

In 1922 noted author Alfred Williams chronicled some of the haunting legends of the upper Thames, including some towns and villages now comprising the borough of Swindon.

In the previous century the local squire in Highworth was famed for his 'eccentric behaviour', including striding the streets committing various acts of self-abasement and humiliation for private improprieties. After his death he was known for walking the streets continuing his acts of penance. It was said that, some time later, the local vicar, bailiff and jurymen set out after the squire's spirit in an attempt to banish it. They apparently conversed with the ghost, who only consented to be trapped if it were in a barrel of apple juice. The rite was done, the barrel sealed and bricked up in the cellar of the squire's former house. In 1922 Williams said this was the last heard of the so-called ghost. However, in our research on Highworth, we found the legend of William Crowdy to be very much alive and well, as reported in the Highworth Tunnels section.

Another Highworth legend relates to an unnamed pub – but distinct from the King and Queen, referenced elsewhere – and concerns the familiar cowled monk being seen in the bar. The landlord was said to have taken out life insurance in case the apparition caused him to have a heart attack!

Alfred Williams's other finding also relates to a local squire; this time 17th-century Squire Parker of the hamlet of Lushill, close to Highworth. This story tells of an elusive stag that was often chased by the squire, but no matter what, the stag always disappeared mysteriously before it was caught. Parker seemed to develop something of an obsession with the stag and, after an unsuccessful day of hunting, swore not to return until he had bagged the antlers of the beast. The other horsemen returned home except for one strange and unknown rider. They pursued the stag together and eventually found it close to the Thames. On grabbing the antlers of the stag, the mysterious horseman and the stag itself 'vanished together in a sheet of flame'. As this story took place centuries before Williams heard it, it is likely to be a simple legend. Legends are often exaggerated tales that seek to serve a warning in line with societal norms. The case for this can clearly be made with the obsessive squire.

The ancient highway that dissects the Roman Ermin Street, the road leading from Blunsdon St Andrew to Highworth, is subject to various ghostly legends. On Forked Elm, halfway between the Cold Harbour and Highworth, a spectral horseman has been seen on several occasions in bygone times. At the same point, the clip-clopping of an invisible horseman is said to follow travellers all the way to the Cold Harbour and then disappear. Two travellers were also said to have seen a man crossing the snowy road one winter, who promptly disappeared without leaving any footprints in the snow. Sams Lane, just off of this road, is said to be haunted by the figure of a child who was hanged in the 17th century for the crime of stealing a sheep.

The road continues as Lady Lane on the other side of Ermin Street. This lane was said to be haunted by a lady: sometimes described as a nun from the nearby, and now demolished, Blunsdon Abbey, and sometimes just as an old lady. The old lady is rumoured to haunt the lane leading down to the church. There are also various accounts of presences felt near to the church itself. Local traditions tell of two presences on separate occasions that vanished upon inspection. Locals have also recounted the legend of a gamekeeper who hanged himself off the church wall in 1906 and is still seen to this day.

Lady Lane in Blunsdon has seen various sightings over the years.

In his 1912 *A Wiltshire Village*, a sizeable book entirely written about the then small village of South Marston, Alfred Williams speaks of two ghosts. The first is a vague rumour of a spot on the avenue where a spirit is said to haunt, due to hidden treasure supposedly buried there. The other ghost is said to be of one Sir Edmund Warneford, a local huntsman. Williams claims that for several generations, the locals reported hearing his galloping up the drive and clearing the high gate at midnight, every night, crying 'Yo ho! Tally ho!' It is said that the weary villagers implored a group of clergymen to lay in wait for Sir Edmund. They confronted him, berated him for his disturbance of the peace and implored him to consent to be laid to rest. Sacrifices and rituals confined his spirit to a pool under a clump of trees; he was to remain there until the pool ran dry. Williams claims that, at the time of writing, Sir Edmund had not been seen again since.

In nearby Hannington village there were several accounts of ghostly monks being seen at the church. It has been speculated this monk might be a Templar Knight buried there in the 12th century. Also in Hannington, in the grounds of the house, a man is said to wonder around, in death, looking for money he had stashed in a secret box and failed to find in life.

The village of Chiseldon, a mile or so south of Swindon town, is rapidly developing houses in the direction of the village. Near to the parish church, a small chapel was said to stand in the grounds of a nearby cottage. The chapel was rumoured to have been destroyed by fire in the 16th century, killing a nun and her dog. Local legend tells that on the night of All Saints' Day each year, the white lady and her dog walk to or from the church, weeping sorrowfully. Witnesses of the lady have reported feeling a sense of 'sorrow and unhappiness'.

In the early 1960s a resident of Chiseldon was walking her dog in a field near to Berricot Lane and found that her dog would repeatedly freeze and tremble. The lady also reported hearing the laughter and voices of children. Thereafter the field was labelled as haunted and strangely enough, in 1969, the field was excavated and the remains of a Roman villa were discovered.

In the 19th century there was a workhouse at the bottom of Strouds Hill where an illegitimate child was born. Had the workhouse authorities found out about the birth, the girl would have been thrown out on the streets. A secret fostering was planned to follow an uneventful birth. However, following complications, the local midwife was called. When the midwife returned with the doctor, to treat the sick mother, the formerly healthy baby was found to be dead: smothered by a pillow. Another cover-up was rumoured to have occurred; the death was recorded as stillborn. At the side of the Washpool the baby was, apparently, buried in a shallow grave. On the baby's birthday a wailing is said to be heard all through the night. Nearby, the shadow-like figure of a woman is said to sob as she searches for the resting place of her child.

A farm at Badbury was said to be the site of an early paranormal investigation. The farmer's wife was said to wake every night to the sound of scuffling sounds and clanking chains in her cowshed. She set her farm workers up in the cowshed overnight to catch the spook. The men fell asleep and woke as the scuffling and clanking of chains started and they quickly fled from their own shadows. Only one farm-hand remained. The man discovered the cows awakening, their binding chains clanking as they stretched, and making scuffling sounds as they tucked into their early morning feed.

Between Chiseldon and Wroughton, the former house of the Calley family at Burderop was said to be home to a traditional grey lady. The lady was said to walk between the house and the old road and passers-by have attempted to speak to her, but she vanished as they did so. Locals describe a woman dressed in a long grey cloak and head covering. Former residents have reported her walking from the former servants' corridors at the back of the house, leaving doors open in her wake.

A member of the Wroughton Women's Institute described an account for Kathleen Wiltshire's *Ghosts and Legends of Wiltshire*. On moving to a new house she saw an old man, bent and passing the window as if he would be coming to the back door. She opened her back door to find no one in the area. This happened several times before she discovered an old man had lived and died in the house. Wroughton is also home to perhaps the most vaguely reported haunting in the borough. Various sources talk of a yew-tree at the top of the hill, which is said to be haunted. They say that walking around the tree three times can raise the spirit.

In the former parish of Rodbourne Cheney, in the centre of urban Swindon, a ghost tale was recounted to Peter Underwood for his book *Hauntings of Wiltshire*. The family legend told of a ghostly coach and four horses appearing once a century, foretelling the death of a family heir. The most recent account was in the 1880s when an heir died a week after a spectral visitation. Conveniently enough, the book *Swindon 50 Years Ago*, penned in 1885, talks of a haunting involving a coach and four horses. The story, told first-hand, took place in 1824 when the coach was seen three times by the witness. A week later his brother died of an acute heart attack.

Also in Rodbourne Cheney a Mrs Dyer – said to be a child-murderer executed in 1896 – is said to walk, in spirit form, from her former cottage to the church, carrying her infant. The sobbing figure is also said to be seen at Newgate, where she was executed. An old vicarage in the area was also rumoured to be haunted by a lady looking for a dead baby, this time in 15th-century dress. Modern legends in the area, discussed on the Internet, talk of a headless horseman and a ghost of an old lady wandering the streets. It is possible that these legends are truncated versions of the traditional ones.

Undocumented oral traditions among Swindonians speak of gallows said to be at a gate on a path between the Princess Margaret Hospital on Okus Road, as was, and the streets off Mill Lane. The site was generally rumoured to be haunted. Surprisingly this rumour was supported, in a text as far back as 1885, talking of the former gallows at Okus fields. The same text tells of a ghost at Pipers Corner on the Coate Road; other written sources suggest this is probably what is now the Pipers Roundabout on Marlborough Road, the road between old Swindon and Coate. At this spot a woman was said to be seen carrying her own head under her arm, or on other occasions carrying a baby in her arms. Another account in the area talks of a tree on Ladder Lane near the old abattoir and Evelyn Street. There was a spot near the tree where grass would not grow and the earth instead formed the shape of a cross. It was said that the groom of Colonel Calley fell here and was killed.

The 1885 account speaks of common, regular and enduring ghost tales, primarily those of private houses where the ghosts have been laid to rest. The Victorian townsfolk of Old Town spoke of the many blocked windows in old houses as being factual evidence of the laying to rest of spirits in those rooms. Also in Old Town the 'old house' of Cricklade Street, for which there are several contenders, was said to have had a ghost in its attic and cellar. Further down the hill, the steps to the cellar of the town hall are said to be haunted by a soldier.

One of the most referenced haunting legends of Swindon refers to Mrs Hedges, who was in her teens in the early 1930s. She was cycling on the Roman Ermin Street between Wanborough and Stratton St Margaret and, midway between the two, a storm broke on a deserted stretch of road. She was said to have spotted a small lane with a thatched cottage at its end. She knocked on the door, seeking shelter, and was accommodated by a silent man. Hedges recalled that there were no sounds within the cottage: the man did not speak and she could not hear the storm when

Could this be the Pipers Corner tree of folklore?

Villet's House – could this be the folkloric 'old house' of Cricklade Street?

inside the cottage. However, her friend insisted there was no cottage on the lane, only a cottage that had been abandoned for 50 years. Some weeks later, Hedges cycled the same route and visited the cottage. She found the cottage as her friend described: derelict, thatch half caved-in, windows broken and the door hanging off its hinges.

The one-time village of Stratton St Margaret, now subsumed by urban Swindon, was said to be haunted by a nun in white who frequented the church, the village and its green. The nun was said to vanish on approach and was rumoured to be connected to a lead-filled skull in the church. The Boundary House was also said to be home to a haunting.

In the middle of the 20th century, a book called *Some Haunted Houses* recounts a strange haunting of Hackham Terrace, a road no longer found on the Swindon street map. It tells of a gigantic naked woman with flesh where her eyes should be, who dematerialised into a rectangle of blue light. Continuing the theme, there are vague reports of people seeing blue hands and arms and blue vapour. In addition, a former establishment in the area, Brown and Plummer, claimed to have the ghost of a man named Lawrence, a former cellar man, in the cellar.

The village and parish of Wanborough, a mile or so south-east of urban Swindon, also has its fair share of haunting accounts. The top of Binlands was said to be the site of the appearance of a Roman soldier. The reporter told of a legionnaire, in full colour, marching straight towards him. Apparently he was agitated and was reluctant to return to the spot. Additionally two houses at Warnage have apparently seen grisly murders, resulting in supposed spirit manifestations. The first related to a David May who died of a gunshot wound. Apparently, until its demolition, locals would tip-toe past the house for fear of waking him up. The second was of a man murdering his son and throwing the body down a well. Rumour suggests his body was a skeleton found under a gallows site at nearby Callas Hill.

At the site of Earlscourt Manor, at nearby Horpit, headless drivers were said to drive carriages to the door. There are vague reports of a botched exorcism of the alleged ghost, in which the exorcists themselves perished. It is said that the haunting of the house started at the time of the Reformation, when monks were turned away from the manor. Apparently the monks prayed that the house should be forever haunted from that point on. Over the years there have been reports of rattling chains, cries, shrieks, doors slamming and faces appearing at windows. One local historian reports that inhabitants would perform rituals and make large donations to the church to keep the spooks at bay.

The legend of the red lady of Hinton Manor has been documented several times over the years and is still repeated on the Internet to this day. The lady was often seen playing a spinet in the house's music room. On at least one occasion, guests have stumbled across the room, drawn to it by the music, and met the lady. Only on repeating the experience to their hosts did they realise the encounter had been unusual.

CONCLUSIONS

Haunted Swindon has presented around 145 cases of alleged hauntings, from the loosest legend to the well-documented current happenings. We hoped this census might be able to tell us something about Swindon's hauntings. However, it is important to remember that this census will not have recorded all hauntings in the town, many of which will remain buried or unreported. Similarly, Swindon might not be representative of hauntings generally. Finally, any analysis involving small numbers of figures should be treated with caution.

The 52 census reports were fully analysed, as only these contained enough information to gain a full picture. The results were somewhat surprising. Firstly, the common perception that 'ghosts only come out at night' must be noted because, contrastingly, while each 'haunting' tended to happen at more than one time of day, it actually turned out that ghost experiences were more common in the afternoon than overnight! In 30 cases, experiencers reported afternoon happenings compared with 25 overnight, 20 in the evening and 13 in the morning.

The age of buildings was another surprise in the analysis. Of the 52 census reports, 50 of which were physical buildings, 19th-century buildings were the most common at 19. But this was closely followed by 20th-century buildings, which came in at 16. Buildings from the 13th to 18th centuries trailed behind with just 12. Admittedly, as pre-Victorian buildings make up the smallest proportion in the borough generally, this should not be a surprise. In relative terms, older buildings are still probably over-represented. Similarly, modern buildings outnumber Victorian buildings possibly several times to one in Swindon. Nevertheless, this does demonstrate that haunting reports are perfectly possible in all buildings, new and old.

A related argument states that rural areas, like ancient towns and cities, report more hauntings than modern urban areas. This is often thought to be because they have the mindset and history to support the tales, and this is sometimes considered to be the reason why towns like Swindon are said to be haunt free. Depending on your definition of rural, our census reports (and overall numbers, similarly) show that the urban haunts outnumber the rural ones by around two to one. Although the borough of Swindon is three-quarters rural, most of the buildings are in urban blocks so, again, this is perhaps not so surprising. But once again this underlines the idea that haunting experiences are perfectly normal in modern, urban settings.

Finally, are we able to conclude which area of Swindon borough has produced more so-called hauntings? As location is easily identifiable we have broken down all 145 accounts by the 21 areas of Swindon, based on municipal ward boundaries. Perhaps not surprisingly, the town centre ward came out on top with 20 accounts. This area comprises mainly Victorian buildings but also includes the town centre. The town centre produced a lot of reports, possibly because of the very public nature of the buildings. With 17, Blunsdon came second. Blunsdon is one of the smallest areas in terms of population, but does cover a large geographic area, taking in villages such as Hannington, Stanton Fitzwarren and South Marston. Many of Blunsdon's accounts were more traditional legends not analysed in the census. In third place were Old Town and Lawn – containing many of the older public buildings of the original Swindon. Most of the hauntings within Old Town and Lawn were focused on the old market town, which is possibly the compact area with the largest number of haunting reports. Wroughton and Chiseldon and the ancient town of Highworth closely followed these, with 14 and 12 respectively. Although most of Highworth is new-build and the ward covers a large geographical area, around half of Highworth's reports came from High Street: possibly the street in the borough with the most ghost reports. With nine reports – mainly of the legend variety – the sparsely populated ward of Ridgeway, set around Wanborough, is worth a mention. The remaining areas of the borough achieved between one and six reports each, with the exception of Dorcan, the only area of town with no reports.

So, are Hauntings Paranormal?

Inevitably the subject of ghosts polarises the interested population into the camps of open-minded rationalists and those led by their belief or disbelief. We respect the beliefs of all, but hope that *Haunted Swindon* has inspired the idea that there is something genuine about haunting experiences but that, in the vast majority of cases, this is not anything paranormal.

Hopefully *Haunted Swindon* has represented a fair cross-section of possible hauntings. These cases seem to demonstrate that most hauntings boil down to the experiencing of unusual but natural events in a spooky context; that is, misattribution through lack of expert knowledge. Consequently, we hope that readers have taken something away from reading this book, as education is often the key to open-minded, rational understanding.

The work of the *Haunted Swindon* project and Paranormal Site Investigators has only just begun. Therefore, if you would like to report an experience please ring us on 0845 652 1529 or visit our website.

Websites of Interest

Paranormal Site Investigators: www.p-s-i.org.uk
Haunted Swindon: www.HauntedSwindon.com
The Orb Zone: www.theorbzone.com
Association for the Scientific Study of Anomalous Phenomena: www.assap.org
Society for Psychical Research: www.spr.ac.uk
PSI at BBC Wiltshire: www.bbc.co.uk/wiltshire
PSI Patron Peter Underwood: www.peterunderwood.org.uk
PSI Historian Ken Taylor: www.wavewrights.com

Glossary of Terms

Anecdotal Evidence

Information that is passed through word of mouth and not scientifically documented. Also paranormal 'evidence' that is collected and recorded in an unscientific or pseudoscientific way.

Anniversary Ghosts

Apparitions, either sentient or insentient, that repeat an action on a certain date or time. For example, a horseman that rides every night at midnight, or a grey lady that makes the same journey once per year.

Anomalous

A deviation from the normal understood order of the world. For example, anomalous phenomena are events that have not been explained and an anomalous photo is a photograph containing an unexplained anomaly.

Apparition

Visions of people (but also animals and objects) that are not present in a material sense. Often these are visions of the dead, but they can be visions of people alive and in crisis.

ASSAP

Association for the Scientific Study of Anomalous Phenomena. A national educational charity formed in 1981 that exists to research, publish and to operate a national network of approved investigators of anomalous phenomena.

Auto-gain Circuit

An automatic circuit, in most domestic recording devices (such as voice recorders or camcorders), whose job is to keep a constant level of sound. When such devices are left alone they turn to 'high gain', thus artificially amplifying background noise. See also EVP.

Belief

See Faith.

Career Experiencers

An experiencer is one who receives or perceives sensory experiences, also known as a percipient. In paranormal terms, this is shorthand for someone who has experienced something they consider to be paranormal. A career experiencer is a person who seems to attract ghostly experiences throughout their life, regardless of whether the location is ordinarily considered haunted.

Clearance

A spiritual mechanism which claims to use various techniques to 'clear' a haunting presence from a house or person.

Coincidence

An incident which feels as if it is purposeful but really takes place by fluke. In paranormal terms, various events are presented as evidence because they look purposeful but, statistically, the likelihood of the incidence could be reasonably expected by chance alone.

Context

Circumstances that surround a particular event, person or location. In paranormal investigative terms, how 'spooky' the context is subjectively perceived to be is important to the report of paranormal experiences.

EMF Meter

A device used to measure typically man-made electromagnetic fields (EMF) such as a mobile phone field and fields caused by electrical currents, for example in power lines or cables. Custom-made EMF meters can also be calibrated to detect weak, complex EM fields that have been shown to trigger hallucinations in a very small number of haunting cases.

Environmental Fluctuations

Any change from the norm in temperature and humidity and any other category of environmental measurement.

ESP

Extra-sensory perception (ESP) is the alleged ability to acquire new information without the use of one of the recognised five senses.

Ethics

In the context of any discipline, profession or subject area, ethics are a codified set of tenets determining what is right and wrong.

EVP

Electronic voice phenomena (EVP) is a form of instrumental transcommunication whereby unknown voices – assumed, usually falsely, to be of persons deceased – are captured using audio recording equipment.

EXIF data

Exchangeable image format extensions hold information on the camera settings that correspond to a particular photo when taken with most digital photographs. EXIF data can be used to ensure digital photographs have not been tampered with and can help to explain anomalies captured.

Expectation

A mental picture, general idea or belief about what will happen in the future. In paranormal terms, the expectation of an individual, especially regarding the perceived existence of the paranormal, can have a profound impact on how ambiguous events are interpreted.

Experiencer

See Career Experiencer.

Extraneous Factors Audit (EFA)

An assessment of a building completed before each paranormal investigation. The EFA establishes any normal factors that could be mistaken for anomalous phenomena either by experiencers, or by environmental or photographic equipment.

Faith

A belief, sometimes religious, in supernatural powers and entities. In some religious traditions, the measure of faith and belief is to accept without the need for any evidence.

Fantasy Prone

Retention of the childhood ability to live fantasies as if they were real. The small proportion of the population of this disposition are prone to experiencing a range of paranormal phenomena.

Folklore

In a ghost story context, the tradition of oral communication of stories that conform with a sense of shared identity or set of norms. Folklore is often representative of certain norms or values, rather than factual accounts of events.

Ghost

A hypothetical entity – often said to be the cause of a haunting – that is associated with various effects, including the sight of apparitions and other phenomena labelled by an individual as paranormal. The entity is believed by some to be the disembodied spirit of a deceased person.

Hallucination

The perception or experience of an event or input that is not objectively present. Hallucinations can be auditory, visual, olfactory, tactile or gustatory. Hallucinations can be caused by a range of triggers, including mental illness, drugs, sleep state (see Hypnagogic and Hypnopompic Imagery), a sense of expectation and ambiguous stimuli and, it is currently believed, various environmental factors (see EMF Meters and Infrasound).

Hoax

A deliberate act designed to fool others into believing the act was genuine. There are various incidents of faked hauntings and ghost evidence, although researchers feel the practice is fairly rare.

Haunted Swindon Project

An educational project set up by educational research charity Paranormal Site Investigators in co-operation with the local authority to uncover and expose the haunted heritage of the borough while promoting rational thought. The project has included paranormal investigations, media exposure, a DVD and book.

Haunting

A series of events – often unconnected and natural in origin – that seem unusual to the experiencer (see Xenonormal) and are attributed to the paranormal, often because of a prior sense of expectation of such an explanation.

Hypnagogic and Hypnopompic Imagery

Respectively, the state of drowsiness before sleep and the state between sleep and being fully awake. Those in such states can experience vivid hallucinations that have often been the cause of sleep-related paranormal events. See also Sleep Paralysis.

Infrasound

Sound of a frequency too low to be audible by the human ear but which, at around 19 hertz, has the potential to cause effects that can be misattributed as paranormal events. Examples include hallucinations in the peripheral vision and the sense of presence. Current evidence suggests that infrasound is a factor in a low proportion of haunting cases.

Investigation

A paranormal investigation is an assessment of specific paranormal claims, often involving interviewing the witnesses of events and trying to assess competing normal causes for those events. Investigations are also used by thrill-seekers as a term for (formal or informal) tourism evenings, and by ghost-hunters for events used to apply pseudoscientific techniques.

Labels

To assign a name to individuals, objects, events or circumstances, especially those with similar features. Labels can be damaging as they are often loaded terms – such as haunting – implying certain features that might not be present in a specific case.

Legends

Traditional stories, sometimes about paranormal events, which are said to contain an element of truth.

Misattribution

To incorrectly relate an event to a particular cause. In psychological terms, whenever an ambiguous event takes place, we relate it to a particular cause. In haunting cases xenonormal events are often misattributed as paranormal.

New House Effect

The theory that, while in a novel environment, the human brain is likely to attend to unusual noises. However, when the environment becomes normal through repeated exposure, the human brain tunes out such noises. This theory is often used to explain unusual sounds heard when moving into a new house, or when visiting a novel environment.

Orb

A two-dimensional anomaly, usually circular and usually pale, typically photographed by digital cameras. Orbs are out-of-focus highlights of light from airborne particles near to the camera lens. Dust can also be represented as moving orbs on video camera. Several people have claimed to see orbs with the naked eye, a likely result of expectation or misattribution of other (nevertheless interesting) phenomena.

Ouija Board

Produced and marketed as a child's toy in the USA in the 1890s. The board is now used by individuals (and unethical researchers in the case of haunting investigations) to attempt to receive messages from dead people.

Paranormal

That which is beyond a normal or scientific explanation. The term can appear loaded, often implying an abnormal cause. Paranormal is often used in a similar way to the term xenonormal: phenomena are only paranormal until normalised.

Parapsychologist

A practitioner of parapsychology. The Parapsychological Association is the professional body for parapsychologists. Full membership depends upon holding a relevant PhD, often in psychology, and being actively engaged in promoting the field. Several UK universities have parapsychological units within their psychology departments. Unaccountably, individuals who take unaccredited, unscientific short courses via the Internet also call themselves parapsychologists.

Parapsychology

A controversial branch of the scientific discipline of psychology that is concerned with the scientific study of anomalous cognition.

Percipient

See Career Experiencer.

Phenomena

Literally, an observable event.

Psychokinesis (PK)

Employment of the power of the mind to move physical objects, formerly telekinesis or mind over matter.

Poltergeist

A hypothetical entity assigned as the cause of particularly overt hauntings. Some believe poltergeists are the spirits of deceased persons. Some parapsychologists believe that a poltergeist is a living agent, often a child or teenager, unknowingly using recurrent spontaneous PK (see Psychokinesis).

Paranormal Site Investigators
PSI is a Wiltshire-based educational charity formed in 2004 whose aim is to conduct research, investigate haunting cases and proactively promote rationalism within the field of ghost research. PSI manages the *Haunted Swindon* Project, publishes a research journal and has completed various projects including TheOrbZone.com

Pseudoscience
That which may closely resemble science but is unscientific, by virtue of being based on false and unscientific assumptions.

Psychic
Paranormal powers or the possessor thereof.

Sceptic
One with a questioning attitude or state of mind. A true sceptic is open-minded and wishes to assess the evidence of unusual or accepted claims. The term is often confused with that of the pathological sceptic, whose attitude is one of close-minded disbelief.

Sleep Paralysis
A terrifying state of paralysis, usually on falling asleep or before waking, where the sufferer often cannot move for several minutes. Sleep paralysis is sometimes accompanied by vivid hallucinations (see Hypnagogic and Hypnopompic Imagery).

Social Desirability
The often unintentional tendency to change our behaviour to gain approval by acting in what is thought to be a socially desirable way. In poorly-controlled interviews this can affect how someone relates their experience. In an investigation context it can affect what an investigator experiences within a group.

Spiritualism
An often informal religious movement centred around the idea that the living can make contact with the dead. See also Faith.

Stone Tape
A 1970s fictional TV play introducing the theory of ghosts that replay in the manner of videotapes. The theory was unfortunately adopted by some researchers.

Superstition
An irrational belief that arises from fear or ignorance. Superstitions are often thought to be practices based on belief or attitude, e.g. not walking under a ladder. In psychology a superstition is also a belief based on faulty evidence that has the tendency to reinforce itself through further faulty evidence.

Trigger Event

The first (often xenonormal) event that takes place within a haunting. Often this event is sufficiently profound for the experiencer to consider a paranormal explanation for the event. The context of the environment often becomes paranormal in perception and a range of xenonormal events often follow to back up the haunting thesis.

UFO

Unidentified flying objects are any objects seen in the sky that cannot be identified by the experiencer. In practice, the term has become almost synonymous with flying saucers piloted by extra-terrestrials.

Xenonormal

The basis for many so-called paranormal events: something that appears to be paranormal but which actually has natural causes that are, at that time, unknown to the experiencer.

Select Bibliography

The number of small historical references generated by *Haunted Swindon* were vast, certainly too many to be noted here. Therefore, this bibliography documents major sources used and can provide further reading for individual haunting accounts. In addition the discussion forums of various websites were used.

Braithwaite, J.J. & M. Townsend 'Sleeping with the entity: A magnetic investigation of an English castle's reputedly haunted bedroom'. *European Journal of Parapsychology*, 20.1, 65-78, 2005.

Child, M. & K. Harry *Local Hauntings*, 1963.

Collins, J. & M. Miller *Chiseldon Memories*, 1994.

Ellis, T. *Ghosts of the South West* http://members.aol.com/MercStG2/GOSWENGPage1.html accessed 10/09/2007.

Evening Advertiser 'Pupils of Commonweal School are Ghost Hunting Again' *Evening Advertiser*, 10/02/1973.

Evening Advertiser 'A Girl Fainted After Being Touched by a Drifting Apparition' *Evening Advertiser*, 05/11/1969.

Evening Advertiser 'Last Orders at the New Inn' *Evening Advertiser*, 13/01/1970.

Evening Advertiser 'Swindon's Clifton Hotel' *Evening Advertiser*', 10/02/1973.

Evening Advertiser 'Weird Lettering' *Evening Advertiser*, 24/04/1977.

Evening Advertiser 'Holy Blazes' *Evening Advertiser*, 02/03/1978.

Evening Advertiser 'Forced Out of Her Home by Ghosts' *Evening Advertiser*, 03/08/1985.

Evening Advertiser 'Haunted House of Penhill' *Evening Advertiser*, 05/08/1985.

Evening Advertiser 'Tourists Trek the Haunted Tunnels' *Evening Advertiser*, 22/09/1989.

Evening Advertiser 'Haunted Health Hydro' *Evening Advertiser*, 02/04/1991.

Evening Advertiser 'A Pub with Real Spirits!' *Evening Advertiser*, 31/10/1994.

Evening Advertiser 'Ghost is Spooked by High Spirits' *Evening Advertiser*, 30/11/1995.

Evening Advertiser 'Ghost Encounter Left Cinema Man Spooked' *Evening Advertiser*, 27/02/1996.

Evening Advertiser 'Has Photographer Snapped a Ghost?' *Evening Advertiser*, 19/02/1996.

Evening Advertiser 'Solved the Mystery of the Haunted Cinema' *Evening Advertiser*, 21/02/1996.

Evening Advertiser 'Going Bump in the Night' *Evening Advertiser*, 22/11/1997.

Evening Advertiser 'Pet Grave Mystery Hides Ghost Story' *Evening Advertiser*, 19/04/1997.

Evening Advertiser 'A Lodger Who Pays no Rent' *Evening Advertiser*, 25/03/1998.

Evening Advertiser 'Haunted House' *Evening Advertiser*, 01/11/2001.

Harrow Inn website About Us http://www.theharrowinnwanborough.com/about%20us.htm accessed 10/11/2007.

Henry, J. (ed.) *Parapsychology: Research on Exceptional Experiences* Routledge, East Sussex, 2005.

Hines, T. *Pseudoscience and the Paranormal* Prometheus Books, US, 1998.

Horowitz, M.J. *Image Formation and Psychotherapy* Jason Aronson, New York, 1983.

Hinton, C. *Wanborough: A Village in All Seasons*, 1987.

Howell, M.A. *Bygone Swindon* Phillimore & Co. Ltd, West Sussex, 1984.

Kurtz, P. *A Skeptics' Handbook of Parapsychology* Prometheus Books: US, 1985.

Levinge, E.M. & R.S. Radway *About Blunsdon: A North Wiltshire Village*, 1976.

Martella, R.C., R. Nelson and N.E. Marchand-Martella *Research Methods* Allyn & Bacon, US, 1999.

Matthews, R. *Haunted Places of Wiltshire* Countryside Books, Berkshire, 2004.

McGovern, U. (ed.) *Chambers Dictionary of the Unexplained: A Guide to the Mysterious, the Paranormal and the Supernatural* Chambers Harrap Publishers Ltd, Edinburgh, 2007.

Morris, W. *Swindon 50 Years Ago* Swindon Advertiser Office, 1885.

Osbourne, A. 'Spirits a Specialty in Relaunched Inn' *Swindon Advertiser*, 08/08/2006.

———— 'Student Spots UFO over Swindon' *Swindon Advertiser*, 13/12/2006.

Paranormal Database Wiltshire – Paranormal Database Records http://www.paranormaldatabase.com/wiltshire accessed 05/08/2007.

Parsons, S.T. and A.R. Winsper 'Infrasound as a Factor in Reported Anomalous, Paranormal & Psychical Experiences Within a Disused Merseyside Shipyard' Proceedings of the 31st International Conference of the Society for Psychical Research 31/08–02/09/07, Cardiff University, UK, 2007.

Perrin, B. 'Hospital Served the Town for 119 Years' *Swindon Advertiser*, 05/12/2007.

Pisa, N. 'Popes Exorcist A-Teams Will Wage War on Satan' *Daily Mail*, 29/12/2007.

Reed, G. *The Psychology of Anomalous Experience* Sentry, US, 1974.

Storr, W. *Will Storr Versus the Supernatural* Ebury Press, 2006.

Swindon Borough Council website The Arts Centre's Resident Ghost http://www.swindon.gov.uk/artsandculture/artscentre/artscentreaboutus/artscentreghost.htm accessed 03/07/2007.

Townsend, M. 'Analysing Paranormal Sound Recordings' *Anomaly: Journal of Research into the Paranormal*, 41, 12-42, 2007.

Townsend, M. 'Are EMF Meters Fit for Purpose?' *Journal of Investigative Psychical Research*, 3(1), 3-4, 2007.

Underwood, P. *Ghosts of Wiltshire* Bossiney Books Ltd, Bodmin, 1989.

Wikpedia Great Western Railway http://en.wikipedia.org/wiki/Great_Western_Railway accessed 10/11/2007.

———— History of Swindon http://en.wikipedia.org/wiki/History_of_Swindon accessed 10/11/2007.

Williams, A. *A Wiltshire Village* Duckworth, London, 1912.

———— *Round About the Upper Thames* Duckworth, London, 1922.

Wiltshire, K. *Ghosts and Legends of the Wiltshire Countryside* Compton Russell Ltd, Wiltshire, 1973.

Wood, D. 'A Life Less Orbinary? Accounts of Experimentation into the Natural Causes of 'Orbs' Anomaly *Journal of Research into the Paranormal*, 40, 17-37, 2007.

Wood, D. and M. Gould 'What's that Noise? An Exploration into the New House Effect' *Journal of Investigative Psychical Research*, 3(2), 8-12, 2007.

Wood, D. and N. Sewell 'Eyewitness Testimony and the Paranormal Investigation: A Rational Perspective *Journal of Investigative Psychical Research*, 1, 2005.

ND - #0299 - 270225 - C0 - 234/156/12 - PB - 9781780913629 - Gloss Lamination